SOMEWHERE TO GO ON SUNDAY

A Guide to Natural Treasures in Western New York & Southern Ontario

by Margaret Wooster

Prometheus Books
Buffalo, New York

SOMEWHERE TO GO ON SUNDAY:
A Guide to Natural Treasures in Western New York and Southern Ontario.
Copyright © 1991 by Margaret Wooster.
Inquiries should be addressed to Prometheus Books, 700 E. Amherst Street, Buffalo, New York 14215, 716-837-2475.

95 94 93 92 91 5 4 3 2 1

Library of Congress Catalog Card Number 90-64251

ISBN 0-87975-634-9

Printed in the United States of America on acid-free recycled paper.

CONTENTS

ACKNOWLEDGMENTS

This book is dedicated to my fellow explorers: Neil and Taylor Schmitz, Suzanne Simon, Gretchen McClintock, Andrew Schmitz, Catherine Parker, Peter and Beth Ruszczyk, Lynda Schneekloth, Bonita Chimes, Sarah Averill, Leah Rowley, Christopher Gerber, and Justin Petrino.

I wish to thank Lester Milbrath, Professor and Director of the gone-but-not-forgotten Environmental Studies Center at SUNY Buffalo, who conceived and made possible the first edition of this book, and who has been Western New York's most steadfast environmental advocate for the past two decades.

Thanks are also due to Prometheus Books for fostering, redesigning, and publishing this second edition of the guide. ■

INTRODUCTION

Since the first edition of *Somewhere to Go on Sunday* was published in 1982, many things have changed in Western New York. For example, Buffalo's parks have been greatly improved with restorations of Frederick Law Olmsted's original buildings and designs. Several new hike/bike trails now link Buffalo to suburban parks and green space. Other natural areas have been added or expanded through the efforts of several public and private conservation organizations such as the Nature Conservancy, the Audubon Society, the Buffalo Museum of Science, and the Department of Environmental Conservation. Also, many individuals have been out there, exploring, delving into the past, and learning the secrets of the land, the Indian namesakes of the creeks, and the legends surrounding certain caves and hilltops. I have tried to incorporate most of these newly accessible places and as much of the lore as possible into this second edition.

The guide describes a range of outdoor places in Western New York and southern Ontario, most of them within an hour's drive from Buffalo. Some of the places are well known, like Niagara Falls, Letchworth, and Allegany State Parks. Many others are known hardly at all—even to longtime residents of the area. A few unlikely places are also included, notably several industrial and postindustrial sites that are historically significant, ecologically important, and simply too colos sal to pass by. The grain elevators, for example, are an impressive part of Buffalo's industrial archaeology that everyone should see.

Among the places not included are amusement parks and most other man-made attractions, and, at the other extreme, certain fragile wilderness environments, which you can discover through affiliation with one of the aforementioned conservation organizations.

Section 1 takes a look first at the lay of the land, then at its subsurface geology, and finally at its weathering through the Ice Age to the early stages of human occupancy. This information is meant to provide a context for "reading" the landscape of Western New York. Any reference to geological formations thereafter may be clarified by consulting this section. ∎

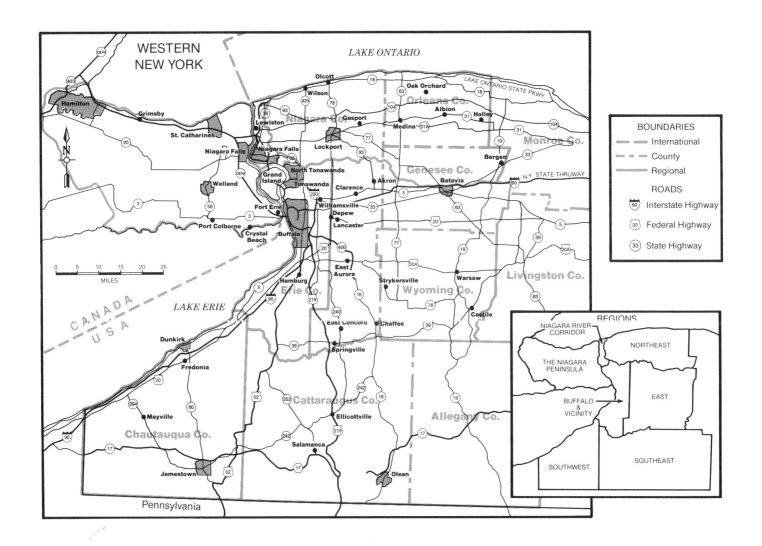

WESTERN NEW YORK

LAKE ONTARIO

Hamilton

Grimsby

QEW

Olcott
Wilson
Oak Orchard
Orleans Co.
Albion
Holley
Medina
Lockport
Gasport
Bergen
Monroe Co.
Lewiston
Niagara Falls
St. Catharines
Niagara Falls
Niagara Co.
Clarence
North Tonawanda
Tonawanda
Grand Island
Welland
Fort Erie
Williamsville
Depew
Lancaster
Akron
Genesee Co.
Batavia
N.Y. STATE THRUWAY
Crystal Beach
Buffalo
Port Colborne
East Aurora
Strykersville
Hamburg
Erie Co.
Warsaw
Wyoming Co.
Livingston Co.
LAKE ERIE
Castile
CANADA
USA
East Concord
Chaffee
Dunkirk
Springville
Fredonia
Ellicottville
Cattaraugus Co.
Allegany Co.
Mayville
Salamanca
Chautauqua Co.
Olean
Jamestown

MILES

Pennsylvania

BOUNDARIES
International
County
Regional

ROADS
90 Interstate Highway
20 Federal Highway
33 State Highway

REGIONS
NIAGARA RIVER CORRIDOR
THE NIAGARA PENINSULA
BUFFALO & VICINITY
NORTHEAST
EAST
SOUTHWEST
SOUTHEAST

WESTERN NEW YORK

Our journey now became wilder every step, the unbroken forest often skirted the road for miles, and the sight of a log-hut was an event. Yet the road was, for the greater part of the day, good, running along a natural ridge, just wide enough for it. This ridge is a very singular elevation, and, by all the enquiry I could make, the favourite theory concerning it is, that it was formerly the boundary of Lake Ontario, near which it passes. When this ridge ceased, the road ceased too, and for the rest of the way to Lockport, we were most painfully jumbled and jolted over logs and through bogs, till every joint was nearly dislocated. (Frances Trollope, Domestic Manners of the Americans, 1832)

Several east-west trending ridges define Western New York's landscape and influenced the pattern of its settlement. The Ridge Road that Frances Trollope traveled in 1831—now Route 104—tracked the southern shore of an extinct glacial lake. Farther south, Route 5, the first coach road to this frontier, followed the Onondaga Escarpment, one of three roughly parallel north-facing ledges formed during the Mesozoic Era when erosion carved away all but the thick uptilted beds of hard limestone. Western New York rises in a series of steps marked by these three escarpments: the Niagara in the north, the Onondaga about 16 miles south of it, and the less clearly defined Portage (or Lake Erie) Escarpment, which forms the northern border of the Allegheny Plateau. From the Ontario Plain, at 246 feet above sea level, the land lifts southward through the Erie and Huron plains to heights of more than 2,000 feet above sea level in the Allegheny Mountains.

Each ascent in tier affects climate (fall comes earlier in the south), vegetation (peach trees grow best in the north), and river flow. Streams that have their headwaters in the Allegheny Plateau—the main

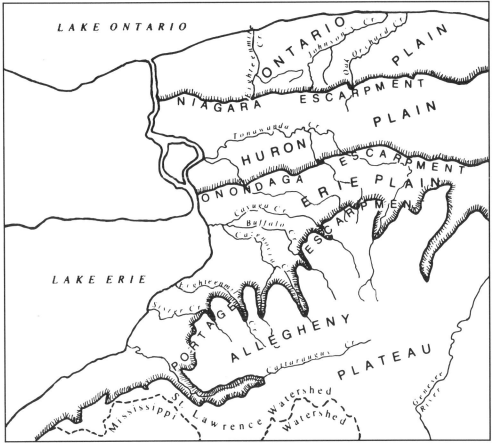

Adapted from Marian E. White, Iroquois Culture History in the Niagara Frontier Area of New York State.

ones are Tonawanda Creek, Buffalo Creek, with its Cayuga and Cazenovia branches, Eighteenmile Creek, and Cattaraugus Creek—flow northward and westward into Lake Erie. The remaining streams—including Niagara County's Eighteenmile, Johnson's, and Oak Orchard creeks—flow north into Lake Ontario.

Soil fertility and drainage also vary with each plain. On the flat, low Ontario Plain the soils are mainly glacial till (rock debris) over lacustrine (lake-bottom) clays and the drainage is poor. Drainage is also generally poor on the Huron Plain, the site of Lake Tonawanda during Western New York's deglaciation. Several large swamps still occupy the area; the State University's Amherst Campus is built on one. About 20 miles east, in an area locally known as the Alabama Swamp, thousands of migrating Canada geese stop every fall and spring to browse in the flooded fields.

South of the Onondaga Escarpment, on the Erie Plain, the soil is fertile, the drainage fair, the surface level, and the climate, tempered by Lake Erie, favorable to most temperate-zone farm crops. Long before the Europeans built their first roads here, the Erie, Wenro, and Neutral Indians were planting squash, corn, and beans on the Erie Plain. Almost all of the known early Iroquois settlements that have been found on the Niagara Frontier were on this plain or along the Niagara River. Later development followed this pattern.

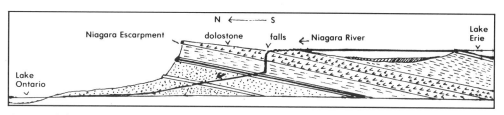

Section of the strata along the Niagara River. North-south distances not to scale. (Adapted from James Hall, Natural History of New York, Part IV: Geology, *1843.)*

GEOLOGY OF NIAGARA FALLS

The Niagara River excavated its own gorge from the Niagara Escarpment, at Queenston-Lewiston Heights, to where the falls are today, over seven miles upstream. The falls, as they are now, represent just one short-lived stage in this continuing erosion. They owe their existence to three basic factors. First, there is a tremendous volume of water involved—Niagara drains four of the Great Lakes. Second, this water must fall from the level of Lake Erie to that of Lake Ontario, a drop of 326 feet. Third, the uppermost or capping rock (Lockport Dolostone), over which the river first fell and still falls, is hard and brittle and is run through vertically and horizontally by clean fractures or "joints"—the result of earth stresses, rivercutting, and

several episodes of glaciation. Water seeps down through these cracks, widening them and eroding the shale beneath. The Lockport Dolostone, thus undermined, breaks off in blocks and falls into the gorge, leaving a perpendicular face.

At its present stage, the cliff at the Horseshoe Falls is 167 feet high. Every year, by a few inches and sometimes by several feet, Niagara's falls recede upriver toward Buffalo. Eventually, when the falls have receded beyond the outcropping dolostone, the river may smooth its bed into a continuing decline of rapids from lake to lake.

The Niagara River originated during the last glacial retreat, 12,000 to 13,000 years ago. As the ice margin moved northward, the glacial lake level fell lower than the Niagara Escarpment, forming ancestral Lake Erie, glacial Lake Iroquois (in the

Ontario basin), and the Niagara River in between. (The Seneca name for Niagara, "Ne-ah-ga," means "neck.") Originally the river fell over the escarpment just above Lake Iroquois's shore at Lewiston. At the same time, Lake Tonawanda formed between the Niagara and Onondaga escarpments as a result of the Niagara River overflow; the incipient Niagara gorge was as yet too small to handle all the river's discharge. Eventually Lake Tonawanda drained through outlets at Holly, Medina, Gasport, Lockport, and "Devil's Hole" near Lewiston, where a notch in the gorge wall marks its channel.

The stratified rock through which Niagara cuts its gorge represents a history that predates the glacial period by hundreds of millions of years. From the high terrace behind the Artpark theater at

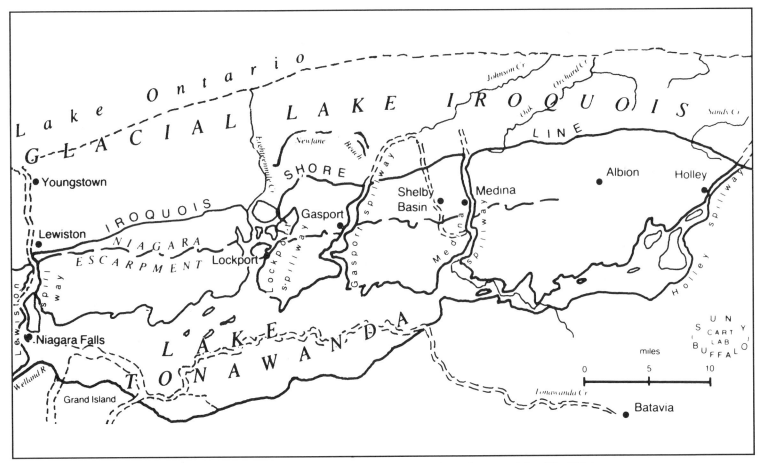

Sketch map of Lake Tonawanda and spillways. (Based on Kindle and Taylor, U.S. Geological Survey Atlas 190, 1913.)

Lewiston Heights, you can see, on the gorge wall opposite, an elegant exposure of the rock beds representing the Paleozoic ("old life") Era. Even from this height (over 250 feet above the river), the red Queenston Shale near the base of the wall can be clearly distinguished from the gray overlying strata. This red-shale formation is the oldest exposed rock face on the Niagara Frontier; it dates from the late Ordovician Period—about 435 million years ago. Estimated to be more than 1,000 feet thick (most of that underground), it was formed from muds supplied over thousands of years by eroding eastern highlands.

GEOLOGY OF ERIE COUNTY

As the Niagara Frontier rises, heading south, the outcrops become younger. Erie County's oldest exposed bedrock, the Camillus Shale, is late Silurian—perhaps 20 million years younger than the Queenston Shale. The Camillus has a high content of salt and gypsum and almost no fossils. It was the bed of a shallow hypersaline sea and indicates a time when the ocean flooding this part of the continent was frequently landlocked. Evaporation under desertlike conditions caused precipitation of salt and gypsum and created an environment in which very little could survive.

Then, a freshening of the water gave rise to an interesting animal, one for which Buffalo is famous among paleontologists. This was the eurypterid or "sea scorpion," an arthropod and relative of the horseshoe crab, which seems to have adapted well to its ambiguous shallow-water environment. The genus *Eurypterus,* found here, had two pairs of eyes, a pair of pincers, a pair of paddlelike appendages, and four pairs of walking legs, indicating that it may have been able to come onto land for brief periods of time. The eurypterid's adaptability gave it a wide geographic range, but good fossil specimens are rare and, after the Silurian Period, completely disappear from this area's geologic record. Eurypterid fossils from the Bertie Formation and Akron Dolostone in Buffalo are exceptionally well detailed; you can see a fine collection of them at the Buffalo Museum of Science.

The Onondaga Limestone marks the beginning of another period of submergence that would last until the end of the Devonian, about 360 million years ago. The clear, warm Onondaga Sea was teeming with animal life. Coral reefs flourished; one exceptionally fine reef was temporarily exposed in Williamsville during Thruway construction. The resulting thick beds of erosion-resistant limestone, along with the eurypterid-bearing strata mentioned above, form the Onondaga Escarpment, the ledge roughly followed by Buffalo's Main Street. Ellicott Creek crosses it at Glen Park, in Williamsville,

ERA	PERIOD		LITHIC TYPES
CENOZOIC 63 m.y.	Quaternary	2 m.y.	Pleistocene Glaciation 0.15 m.y.a.–2 m.y.a.
	Tertiary	61 m.y.	
	— 63		
MESOZOIC 177 m.y.	Cretaceous	75 m.y.	GEOLOGIC TIME SCALE
	— 138		
	Jurassic	67 m.y.	Patterned areas indicate strata record in N.Y.
	— 205		
	Triassic	35 m.y.	
	— 240		
PALEOZOIC 330 m.y.	Permian	50 m.y.	Unpatterned areas indicate absence of record in N.Y.
	— 290		
	Pennsylvanian	40 m.y.	
	— 330		
	Mississippian	30 m.y.	m.y.a. = millions of years ago
	— 360		
	Devonian	50 m.y.	
	— 410		
	Silurian	25 m.y.	Strata exposed in Niagara Gorge
	— 435		
	Ordovician	65 m.y.	
	— 500		
	Cambrian	70 m.y.	Dates from U.S. Geological Survey. Adapted from Tesmer (1981).
	— 570		

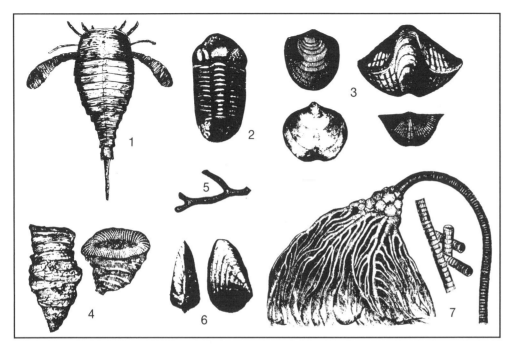

Common fossils of Western New York: (1) Eurypterid. (2) Trilobite. (3) Brachiopods (four species). (4) Corals (two species). (5) Bryozoa. (6) Pelecypod. (7) Crinoid (inset shows stem segments).

and makes a pretty waterfall. Murder Creek spills over farther east at Akron Falls Park. The City of Buffalo's only waterfall is in Forest Lawn Cemetery, just west of Main Street, where Scajaquada Creek crosses the escarpment.

Three hundred feet of black and gray shales—the Hamilton group—succeed the Onondaga Limestone. Another major land uplift in the continental northeast (the Acadian orogeny) activated rivers that carried off debris from the new highlands and deposited it in the seas here, turning them muddy. The black bituminous shales of the early deposits (Marcellus Formation) indicate that stagnant water supported some plants and a limited variety of animals. Succeeding gray shales and occasional thin beds of limestone in the Hamilton Group reveal a changing environment, sometimes conducive to animal life, sometimes not, and sometimes only to a few species that proliferated and diversified. Strata immediately above and below the Tichenor Limestone (prominent along the gorge of Eighteenmile Creek and, near its mouth, in the beach cliffs of Lake Erie) are especially fossiliferous. Corals, bryozoans, brachiopods, pelecypods, crinoids, and trilobites are commonly found. Concretions, globular rock aggregates usually formed around a fossil core, are also abundant. (If you freeze one and then drop it into boiling water, the fossil may hatch out perfectly.) Brachiopods and trilobites thrived, judging by their numbers, in the muds that are now the shale beds of Smoke's Creek. Huge colonies of crinoids or "sea lilies" must have existed during the brief periods of clear water, for several bands of limestone are almost entirely composed of crinoid stems. At Spring Creek, in the Town of Alden, dwarfed and pyritized specimens of most of the common fossils in Erie County indicate a temporary lagoonal environment unfavorable to normal animal growth.

Again, Late Devonian seas often must have been muddy to the point of stagnation, since the several hundred feet of Upper Devonian shale beds are almost devoid of fossils. Occasionally someone comes upon an armored fish, such as the *Dinichthys magnificus* found at Eighteenmile Creek and now on display in Buffalo's science museum.

The uppermost Devonian rock is siltstone, a coarser sediment marking the area's proximity to

land. From this time on, that is, during the rest of the Paleozoic, as well as during the Mesozoic and Cenozoic eras, Western New York was above sea level and subject to erosion.

During the 177 million years of Mesozoic times, streams eroded Western New York into a low plain. No record exists here of the changing landscape or of the dinosaurs that dominated the era. Then, in the Tertiary Period (about 63 million years ago), there was another radical movement in the earth's crust. The plain of Western New York

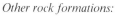

Other rock formations:
(1) Septarium concretion.
(2) Concretion with fossil.
(3) Cone-in-cone concretion.
(4) Crinoidal limestone.

was tilted up gently toward the south to form the Allegheny Plateau. This land rise activated the once sluggish flatland rivers, and the rate of erosion increased, contributing to the high relief of the southern tier. Present-day land contours partly originated in this Tertiary landscape.

However, most of the details of our present topography resulted from glacial events in the Pleistocene Epoch, beginning about two million years ago. The Laurentide Ice Sheet, which covered central and eastern Canada and the northern United States, including most of New York State, advanced and receded in at least four stages. It was the last Wisconsin stage (about 100,000 to 10,000 years before the present) that finalized the impression on New York's topography. Up to 10,000 feet thick in central Canada, the glacier weighted down the land it covered. This, along with its smoothing, grinding, crushing, carrying, and depositional work, determined the present boundaries of lakes Erie and Ontario and the consequent flow of the Niagara River between. Hundreds of smaller lakes (Lime, Crystal, and Java lakes, for example) resulted when large blocks of glacial ice melted, creating depressions in the enclosing gravels. Lake Chautauqua developed when glacial drift dammed a northwestward-trending stream valley; the Finger Lakes in central New York were formed in the same way.

The ice sheet's retreating edge left several end-moraine systems (ridges of debris) across Western New York. Conspicuous among these are the Lake Escarpment system, stretching through Chaffee, Springville, and Gowanda; and the Hamburg Moraine, whose sharp knolls and enclosed basins extend from the Hamburg fairgrounds northeast to Batavia.

Glacial deposits blocked the ancestral Allegheny River (which, before glaciation, flowed north from Randolph through the Gowanda area into the Lake Erie Basin) and created the new drainage divide between the Mississippi and the St. Lawrence watersheds. The present-day Allegheny drains south into the Ohio River and thence into the Mississippi. Evidence of this last change can be seen at the Gowanda end of the Zoar Valley. There Cattaraugus Creek occupies a deep gorge inherited from the ancestral Allegheny.

When deglaciation finally did occur, it was a fairly rapid process. By about 12,000 years ago, New York was ice free. Spruce forests reclaimed the landscape. Woolly mammoths, mastodons, musk oxen, barren-ground caribou, and dire wolves repopulated the forests. As the spruce forests gave way to pine and then birch and hardwood forests, other species of mammals became dominant—woodland caribou and bison, ground sloths, peccary, giant beaver, and bear—all of which are extinct or locally absent today. By at least 8,000 years ago, humans had arrived on the scene.

INDIAN HISTORY IN WESTERN NEW YORK

People may have moved into Western New York as soon as it became accessible after the glacier's retreat. Early Archaic projectile points from the Lockport area indicate that Paleoindians were here perhaps 8,000 years ago. Projectile points found along glacial lakeshores and radiocarbon-dated charcoal from various sites have established Paleoindian presence in southeastern New York 10,000 years ago. Conditions permitting, it was probably not long until they made their way here.

One early habitation site—Riverhaven 2—is on the east side of Grand Island along the Niagara River. Remains from the band of about fifty people who lived there sometime between 1000 and 600 B.C. indicate that they hunted, fished, gathered wild plants, and traded with neighbors along the main water routes. At another prehistoric site—Divers or Spirit Lake, just north of Batavia—large amounts of Onondaga Limestone were quarried and worked into points that have been found throughout the state. Numerous burial mounds have been found in Western New York; one, the Lewiston mound, can be seen at Artpark in the woods across the road from parking lot D. Tonawanda Island, at the mouth of Tonawanda Creek in the Niagara River, was also a mound site.

Agricultural village sites containing pottery, tools, and sometimes earthwork protection barriers date from around 1400. The slash-and-burn agricultural practice of these early Iroquoians meant they had to move their villages every 15 to 25 years to find fresh sources of fertile soil, firewood, and game. This has made it difficult to arrive at a definite sequence for the Neutral, Erie, and Wenro settlements that were in Western New York at various times prior to 1655.

By 1655 the Iroquois ("Ho-de-no-sau-nee" or "people of the longhouse") had pushed westward into the Niagara Frontier and displaced the last of the local tribes. This then became the hunting territory of the Seneca, the westernmost of the five-nation confederacy, whose main villages were in the Genesee Valley until 1779, when American colonists, under General John Sullivan, destroyed them.

With the help of their British allies, the Seneca moved into Western New York. The British positioned the new villages in a strategic line along the frontier, from the Cattaraugus in the south, to the Tuscarora in the north. About 1,600 Seneca settled along Buffalo Creek, in what is now South Buffalo. By spring 1781, the Indians were planting the clearings above the creek flats using British hoes and seed corn. Nineteenth-century histories tell how, in 1800, old Sgan-dyiuh-gwa-deh (after whom Scajaquada Creek was named) preceded the Buffalo Creek reservation surveyor from tree to tree, carefully excluding undesirable land. (All of what later became Tifft Farm was excluded.)

It was here, at Buffalo Creek, that the Six Nation Iroquois (the Tuscarora, forced out of North Carolina, joined the five nations in 1714) held many of their councils—first with the British, later with the Americans—to determine future boundaries of their land. Red Jacket, the famous Senecan orator, was a major figure in these negotiations. In his red coat (a gift of the British Crown) and his plate-sized silver medal (a gift of President Washington), Red Jacket is himself an allegory of Senecan history on the Niagara Frontier—a history of embroilment in the white man's wars, through which the Indians steadily lost territory.

By the time Buffalo was incorporated as a city in 1832, the Iroquois had sold all their land west of the Genesee except for

Sa-Go-Ye-Wat-Ha (Red Jacket), Seneca Sachem. (Courtesy Buffalo and Erie County Historical Society)

the Allegany, Cattaraugus, Tuscarora, Tonawanda, and Buffalo Creek reservations. In 1842, the Ogden Company succeeded in buying the last. They sold 5,000 acres along Buffalo Creek to the Ebenezer "Community of True Inspiration," a spiritual sect from Germany who formed a communal society and ran farms and sawmills on the land for 20 years before selling it off in parcels and moving to Iowa. Street names and a historical marker on Buffam Street (off Seneca) are about all that remain to commemorate the Iroquois settlement on Buffalo Creek.

The rest is a history too detailed and too often told to retell here. A selected list of later Buffalo and Western New York histories can be found in the Bibliography. ∎

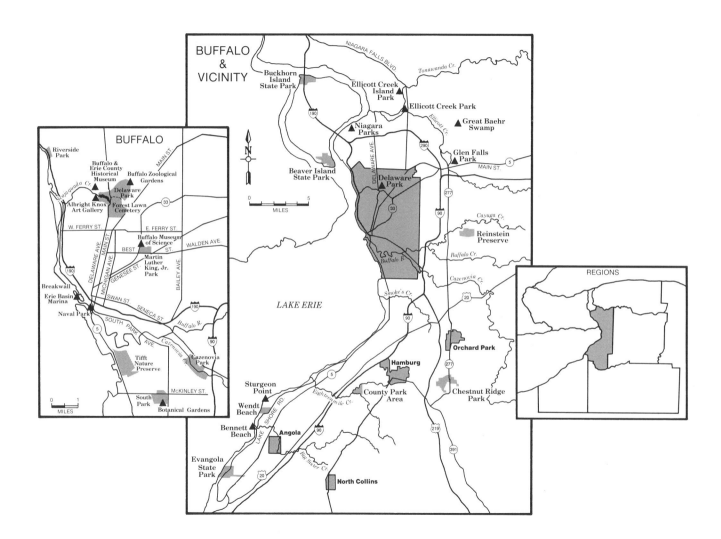

BUFFALO & VICINITY

BUFFALO

REGIONS

Riverside Park
Buffalo & Erie County Historical Museum
Buffalo Zoological Gardens
Delaware Park
Albright Knox Art Gallery
Forest Lawn Cemetery
E. FERRY ST.
W. FERRY ST.
MAIN ST.
Buffalo Museum of Science
BEST ST.
WALDEN AVE.
Martin Luther King, Jr. Park
DELAWARE AVE.
MICHIGAN AVE.
GENESEE ST.
BAILEY AVE.
Breakwall
Erie Basin Marina
Naval Park
SWAN ST.
SENECA ST.
SOUTH PARK AVE.
Buffalo R.
Cazenovia Cr.
Tifft Nature Preserve
Cazenovia Park
McKINLEY ST.
South Park
Botanical Gardens
MILES
0   1

Buckhorn Island State Park
NIAGARA FALLS BLVD.
Tonawanda Cr.
Ellicott Creek Island Park
Ellicott Creek Park
Great Baehr Swamp
Ellicott Cr.
Niagara Parks
Glen Falls Park
MAIN ST.
Beaver Island State Park
DELAWARE AVE.
Delaware Park
Cayuga Cr.
Reinstein Preserve
Buffalo Cr.
Buffalo R.
Cazenovia Cr.
LAKE ERIE
Smoke's Cr.
N
MILES
0   5
Orchard Park
Hamburg
Chestnut Ridge Park
Sturgeon Point
County Park Area
Wendt Beach
LAKE SHORE RD.
Eighteenmile Cr.
Bennett Beach
Angola
Big Sister Cr.
Evangola State Park
North Collins

BUFFALO & VICINITY

CITY PARKS

Frederick Law Olmsted began designing Buffalo's park system in 1868 with the 350-acre "Park" (now Delaware Park) in the north quarter of the city as its focus. Eventually, broad tree-lined parkways connected this park to Parade (now Martin Luther King, Jr. Park) on the east side and to Front Park on the west. Wide avenues for private carriages were flanked on both sides by generous strips of green park, which provided pedestrian paths and created outside lanes for commercial traffic. Olmsted's strategy was for this chain of parks and greenways to so integrate the city's commercial and residential districts with its pleasure grounds that all neighborhoods would have easy access to "scenes of sylvan beauty."

Olmsted wanted a south park, with recreational waterways and beach front, to be located just beyond the southern city-line on the lakeshore. This park would join to the Buffalo system by way of a grand viaduct over the railroad yards that crowded the Buffalo River. Parkways were to be extended into the neighborhoods of South Buffalo. Olmsted's firm also presented plans for a riverside park that would make use of another of Buffalo's obvious recreational resources: the Niagara River. A footbridge over the Erie

Canal would connect the park to the riverbank, where there would be paths, a boat landing, and a pergola.

Parts of Olmsted's park system never materialized, others have disappeared with time. For example, instead of the lakeshore area the architect had chosen, Buffalo allocated two smaller inland sites—present-day South Park and Cazenovia Park. The grand viaduct to connect the Buffalo and South Buffalo systems was never built. In the mid-1960s, the part of Humboldt Parkway between Martin Luther King, Jr. and Delaware parks was sacrificed for the Kensington Expressway. Riverside Park lost its access to the river with the construction of the Thruway.

Wherever Olmsted's design remains, however, its beauty is apparent. The Bidwell, Chapin, and Lincoln parkways on Buffalo's west side are still impressive, though the elms that once graced them are gone. Delaware Park's meadow (now a golf course and playing fields) illustrates Olmsted's belief that recreational spaces should also please the eye. For contrast, Olmsted "planted out" the section of the park south of Delaware Lake, creating woods with quiet paths and secluded picnic spots.

Today, Buffalo's parks are still undergoing changes. Thanks to citizen groups like the Buffalo Friends of Olmsted Parks, the Scajaquada Pathway Committee, and others, many changes are for the better. Recent improvements include restoration of Olmsted's original arboretum design for South Park, restoration of the turn-of-the-century casinos at Delaware and Cazenovia Parks, and the creation of new linkages such as the Scajaquada Pathway between Delaware Park and Riverwalk.

Delaware Park is still, as Olmsted planned it to be, the central park of the city. Perhaps it was never more central than now with the profusion of walkers, joggers, bicyclists, roller skaters, roller skiers, stroller pushers, and others who can be seen on any summer evening circling the Ring Road for exercise, air, and the general promenade. There are basketball, tennis, and lawn-bowling courts, an 18-hole golf course, baseball diamonds, soccer fields, a bridle path, and children's playgrounds—the most extensive being the Tot Lot, near Parkside Avenue. The 1.8-mile Ring Road circles the meadow and has a juice bar (The Juicery, near Meadow Road) where you can buy fruit drinks and veggie snacks in the summertime. On the west side of Delaware Avenue, which cuts the park in two, are Delaware Lake and the Casino, designed by Green and Wicks in 1900 and recently renovated. Here also are the best hills for winter sledding. From June through August, Shakespeare in the Park is performed in the natural amphitheater above the lake.

The Albright Knox Art Gallery and the Buffalo and Erie County Historical Museum (the only building left from the 1901 Pan-American Exposition) both overlook the park. The gallery is open Tuesday through Saturday, 11 to 5; Sundays and holidays, 12 to 5. The museum is open Tuesday through Saturday, 10 to 4. Fees in both places are voluntary.

Red Jacket's monument in Forest Lawn Cemetery.

Forest Lawn Cemetery: Olmsted chose the site for Delaware Park, in part, because of its proximity to Forest Lawn, which visually extends the open space. But it is clear that the cemetery itself was designed to be recreational as well as burial grounds. Stone walks and amphitheaters surround spring-fed ponds; hills afford grand views across Delaware Lake.

Once the farm of Erastus Granger, the cemetery was dedicated in 1866, according to a Masonic monument atop a distinctive earth mound near the chapel. Much of the city's history is present here. There are memorials to Millard Fillmore and Ely S. Parker of national fame; to Sarah Hinson, Jesse Ketchum, and other Buffalo notables; and to Red Jacket along with some of the other Native Americans whose bones were removed from their original resting place near Buffam Street and Buffalo Creek. Red Jacket's monument, with its sad inscription, and the famous Blocher and Birge Memorials are all to be seen. Jubilee Spring, Buffalo's water supply at the turn of the century (before the present-day intake was put at the mouth of Lake Erie), still flows in Forest Lawn, as does Scajaquada Creek.

Martin Luther King, Jr. Park:

Located at Fillmore and Best Streets,

"WHEN I AM GONE AND MY WARNINGS ARE NO LONGER HEEDED, THE CRAFT AND AVARICE OF THE WHITE MAN WILL PREVAIL. MY HEART FAILS ME WHEN I THINK OF MY PEOPLE, SO SOON TO BE SCATTERED AND FORGOTTEN."

Martin Luther King, Jr. Park, once called Humboldt Park, is another green space we owe to Olmsted's vision. An old carriage route still partially surrounds the park, protecting it from busy city streets. A central feature is the fountain and magnificent 500-foot-diameter wading pool. There are also picnic shelters and, a recent addition, a bust of Martin Luther King, Jr. Adjacent to the park is the Buffalo Museum of Science, open daily from 10 to 5 and some evenings.

Riverside Park is at

Buffalo's northwest city-line (Niagara, Tonawanda, and Crowley Streets). The Irene Gardner Pedestrian Bridge, named after the resident who fought for it, connects Riverside Park to the Niagara shore, Riverwalk, and the Ontario Street fishing area, which can also be reached from the foot of Ontario Street. This is a convenient place to watch the river roll by (here it is near its widest), or to drop a line for panfish, bass, or pike. Riverside Park also has an outdoor swimming pool and an ice-skating rink.

Cazenovia Park: According to research

by the Buffalo Friends of Olmsted Parks, Cazenovia Park, in South Buffalo, once had a large lake, formal flower gardens, and a casino whose open terraces teemed with strolling couples. The park has suffered the ravages of time and progress. However, at this writing, the Casino is being restored to its original appearance, as designed by Esenwein and Johnson in 1916.

Cazenovia Creek flows through the park. It is named after Theophile Cazenove, a land agent for the Holland Land Company, who acquired 3.3 million acres of Western New York in the 1790s. The park is a good place to put in a canoe and paddle down to the creek's confluence with the Buffalo River, and downstream six more looping river-miles to Lake Erie. (The return trip is no more arduous as there is little current in the Buffalo River.)

Take Route 190 to Seneca Street, and Seneca Street south to Cazenovia Street. The park is at the end of the street.

South Park and Conservatory (Buffalo and Erie County Botanical Gardens): Located at McKinley Parkway and South Park Avenue (across from Our

Lady of Victory Basilica), South Park was originally designed by Olmsted as an arboretum and was planted with 2,300 species of trees and shrubs. Although many of these have been lost, restoration of the South Park Arboretum has begun with a 1.25-acre Shrub Garden, designed to display shrubbery hardy to Western New York and complete with winding paths and benches.

South Park's main attraction is the three-domed conservatory, built in 1898 by the greenhouse firm of Lord and Burnham in the vogue of London's famous Crystal Palace. Composed of 12 houses, the conservatory features a 67-foot-high palm dome, a skywalk and waterfall, a children's learning garden, a cactus house, specimen orchids, bromeliads, ferns, fruit trees, and brilliant displays of flowering plants that change with the seasons. Open from 9 to 4 every day, including holidays. No fee.

Buffalo Zoological Gardens: The

23-acre zoo is on the north side of Delaware Park; its main entrance faces the meadow. It began, in Olmsted's design, as a deer park, but, as more animals were donated over the years, buildings became necessary and were constructed whenever enough funds could be raised. Bear pits designed to look like Roman ruins were built in 1898. In 1912 "Frank," the African elephant, was finally untied from his tree and ensconced in the brand-new (present-day) elephant house. The main animal house was built in the 1930s under direction of Roosevelt's Work Projects Administration. WPA artists also carved the stone

animal sculptures at the gates and the stone bas-reliefs around the outside windows of the main building. A giraffe house and children's zoo were added in the 1960s. More recent additions include a tropical habitat for lowland gorillas, an outdoor exhibition area for the big cats, a visitor center, and a science magnet school.

One of the most pleasant things about the zoo is its layout—a symmetrical arrangement of paths focusing around a prairie dog city. Outside paths take you past antelope, bison, camels, elk, gemsbok, zebra, llamas, and reindeer. The zoo is open seven days a week from 10 to 5:30 (4:30 in winter). It is closed Thanksgiving Day and Christmas Day. Strollers are available at the entrance. Admission fee.

Tifft Nature Preserve, of all of Buffalo's

green spaces, most symbolizes the emergent environmental awareness of our time and the dilemmas it poses to those in urban-industrial areas. To appreciate just how hopeful and key a place it is, we must learn a little of its history.

Originally a wetland with no recognized value, this several-hundred-acre area between the Buffalo River and the lake-shore, was bought by George Washington Tifft in the 1840s. A dairy farm and, later, stockyards were established on the uplands. These grew and thrived, strategically located as they were near both the port and the growing city market. In the 1870s Tifft Farm was sold to Lehigh Valley Railroad. After an extensive system of canals was dug connecting the railroad yards to Buffalo's harbor, the Tifft area became,

and remained through the early 1900s, a major transfer point for Great Lakes shipping. However, antitrust legislation, a disastrous fire at the large freight house, and a slowed economy caused Lehigh Valley to abandon Tifft in the 1930s. Many people today recall how it was in the succeeding decades: a hobo camp, a dump that was always burning. During that period, the City of Buffalo acquired the property and sold it, in 1955, to Republic Steel, which used the site to dump slag.

In the early 1970s, Tifft Farm was selected to be the repository for two million cubic yards of solid waste that had to be removed from Squaw Island where the Buffalo Sewer Authority planned to build a new treatment plant. However, by now the aboriginal Tifft—marsh, wildlife habitat, migratory bird stopover—had gained some advocates: notably Tony Pierzchala, a young man who knew and loved it as a wild area. Through his and others' efforts, a compromise plan was reached with the city (which once again owned the site): the waste would be moved, but the wetlands and wildlife would be saved and the area made into an urban nature preserve. The transferred waste was sculpted into four mounds in a 40-acre area at the southwest corner of the preserve. Clay walls and an elaborate drainage system were installed to protect adjacent water from leachate. The mounds were covered with two feet of soil and planted with wildflower and grass seed. A 20-acre pond was created as a result of this excavation.

Today, the 264-acre nature preserve features six miles of hiking trail, a 75-acre marsh with a boardwalk from which many of the migrating birds that stop here can be seen, and three ponds named after Pierzchala's three daughters. Red fox, beaver, muskrats, cottontails, and raccoons are among the permanent residents. The log-

cabin Makowski Visitor Center provides trail maps and displays of local plants and animals. Guides conduct bird-watching and nature walks regularly as well as outdoor education classes for children of all ages. In winter you can follow the trails on snowshoes or cross-country skis.

Tifft is administered by the Buffalo Museum of Science and is open from 9 to 5 daily except on major holidays. No entrance fees.

To get there, take Route 5 to Fuhrmann Boulevard and get off at the Tifft Street exit. Follow signs.

WATERFRONT

Buffalo River: The Buffalo River and neighboring South Buffalo became the city's industrial center after the western end of the Erie Canal was completed there in 1825 (no trace of that terminal remains). Great Lakes steamers carrying grain, lumber, livestock, and iron stopped here while their cargo was transferred to canal boats and freight trains bound for eastern seaports. Flour mills, grain elevators, tanneries, and foundaries grew up along the river's banks and lakeshore, followed by steel mills and related industries. By the 1920s, Buffalo was the second-largest steel producer in the nation.

Buffalo lost its port advantage with the construction of the Welland Canal and the St. Lawrence Seaway, which allowed Great Lakes traffic to bypass this city completely. The Buffalo River bears both the scars and the monuments of this industrial past.

A canoe trip up the river, beginning at the Erie Basin Marina at the river's mouth, takes you through canyons of grain elevators, most of them empty relics of an era when the Queen City was a collection point on the Great Lakes for midwest grain. Fields of wild wheat surround some of the elevators and abandoned rail lines; great blue heron, snipe, and other waterfowl may be seen where the banks have natural-

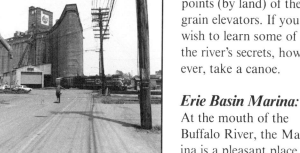

ized. Invisible now, but imaginable on the quiet river, are earlier occupants: the Seneca who moved here in the 1780s after their Genesee Valley villages were burned by the colonial army; and, before them, in that obscure time prior to European contact, the Erie, who built a circular fort upstream, on the south bank of Buffalo Creek.

To get to the river by car, take Seneca Street to Michigan Avenue. Go south on Michigan to Ohio Street. Ohio takes you along the river to St. Clair and then Childs Street, affording some of the best vantage points (by land) of the grain elevators. If you wish to learn some of the river's secrets, however, take a canoe.

Erie Basin Marina: At the mouth of the Buffalo River, the Marina is a pleasant place to catch the breezes off the lake on a hot summer's day. The

small park has an observation tower, a restaurant, picnic tables, flower gardens, plenty of parking, and, of course, docking facilities for small boats. If you don't own a boat, you can take a cruise on the 70-foot sightseeing yacht, *Miss Buffalo,* which provides two-hour tours from the Marina through the harbor, the river, and the Black Rock Canal. It sails seven days a week, from June through September. For fees and times, call 716-856-6696.

Take Swan Street west to Erie Street, then follow the Marina signs.

Buffalo and Erie County Naval and Servicemen's Park:

Next to the Erie Basin Marina and connected to it by Riverwalk, the park is homeport for the guided missile cruiser *Little Rock,* a destroyer called *The Sullivans,* and a submarine, the *Croaker.* The small museum houses a

model ship collection. A 10-minute video introduces the park, which opens daily at 10 A.M., from April 1 to October 31. There is an admission fee. Fore more information call 716-847-1773.

Breakwall (Bird Island Pier):

Situated just downstream from the Peace Bridge and the Lake Erie outlet to the Niagara River, this mile-long barrier separates the fast-flowing river from the Black Rock Canal. Boaters, including the West Side Rowing Club, use the quiet waters of the canal. Anglers fish from the breakwall and along the river shore of Bird Island, where the breakwall is anchored. The skyscapes from here are spectacular when weather and light permit.

Take West Ferry across Niagara Street and the lift bridge over the canal to Bird Island.

BICYCLE & PEDESTRIAN PATHWAYS

Riverwalk: Buffalo's system of "hike and bike" trails is growing. Riverwalk, a two-lane asphalt path for walkers and bicyclists, stretches 14 miles along the Erie-Niagara shore—from the Marina at the mouth of the Buffalo River, to Tonawanda Creek (the Barge Canal) in the City of Tonawanda. Eventually it will be tied to the Scajaquada Pathway, now completed from Nottingham Terrace to Grant Street, and to trails along Ellicott and Tonawanda Creeks in the Town of Amherst.

Scajaquada Pathway: The Scajaquada Pathway is a good example of how Olmsted's concept of green space and greenways within the city can be extended. A new connection between Delaware Park and Riverwalk, the pathway will eventually link central Buffalo to some 20 miles of continuous riverside trail. It has also helped bring long-neglected Scajaquada Creek back into the city's consciousness.

Until recently, Scajaquada Creek was hidden from sight in the city. Three and a

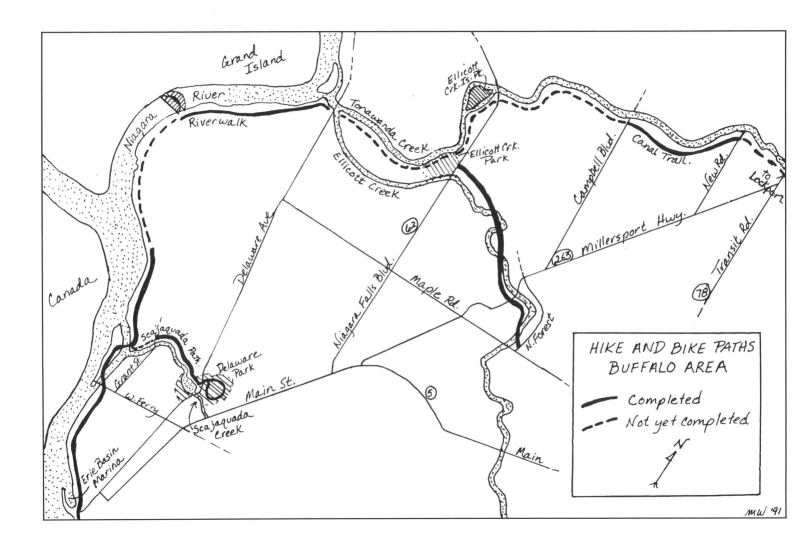

Grand Island

Niagara River

Riverwalk

Canada

Tonawanda Creek

Ellicott Crk. Is. Pk.

Ellicott Creek

Ellicott Crk. Park

Campbell Blvd.

Canal Trail

New Rd.

to Lockport

Delaware Ave.

62

263 Millersport Hwy.

78

Transit Rd.

Niagara Falls Blvd.

Maple Rd.

N. Forest

Scajaquada Path

Grant St.

Delaware Park

W. Ferry

Main St.

Scajaquada Creek

Erie Basin Marina

5

Main

HIKE AND BIKE PATHS
BUFFALO AREA

——— Completed

– – – Not yet completed

N

MW '91

half miles of it were tunneled underground and tied into the city's sewer system in the 1920s. The creek surfaces in Forest Lawn Cemetery, just west of Main Street. There one can see waterfalls where it crosses the Onondaga Escarpment and hear a wide variety of songbirds, which dwell among the overgrown banks. Downstream the creek was all but buried under the Scajaquada Expressway. The newly completed pathway gives new visibility and access to this section of Scajaquada.

Scajaquada comes from the phonetic pronunciation of "Sgandyiuh-gwa-deh," also spelled "Scaugh-juh-quatty" and "Conjockety" in the old Buffalo histories. Phillip Conjockety was an adopted Seneca, "the last survivor of the

Painting of Phillip Conjockety, 1862. (Courtesy Buffalo and Erie County Historical Society)

ancient Neutral Nation," and a man of great influence. After the Revolutionary War, he persuaded the Seneca Nation to remain on this side of the Niagara, instead of joining other Iroquois in Canada. He helped Red Jacket survey the Buffalo Creek Reservation boundary in 1800.

During the War of 1812, "Conjockety Creek" was the American's first line of defense against the British, who after landing at Black Rock (near the creek's mouth) fought their way south to the village of Buffalo and set it on fire.

Ellicott Creek Bicycle Path: This six-mile-long bicycle and hiking trail follows Ellicott Creek between North Forest Road and Niagara Falls Boulevard. It was constructed as part of the U.S. Army Corps of Engineers flood-control project on Ellicott Creek, completed in 1988, which reduced the creek's 100-year floodplain in the Town of Amherst by about 90 percent. The pathway follows the creek through the SUNY Buffalo campus and then parallels the constructed overflow channel west to Niagara Falls Boulevard. You may cross the Boulevard at the stoplight here and continue pedaling another mile or so along the creek through Ellicott Creek Park (see p. 32). Ellicott Creek is named after Joseph Ellicott, chief surveyor and land agent for the Holland Land Company.

Take Maple Road to North Forest. Turn north on North Forest and park in the parking area on the left (the second driveway from the corner). There are signs directing you to the trail.

Amherst Canal Trailway follows Tonawanda Creek (the Barge Canal), in the Town of Amherst, from New Road to Campbell Boulevard and is currently being extended to Ellicott Creek Island Park at Niagara Falls Boulevard. Erie County has plans to join both this trail and the Ellicott Creek bike path with Riverwalk.

GRAND ISLAND & THE TONAWANDAS

Beaver Island State Park: The main attraction of this 900-acre park is its beach, which (be forewarned) on summer weekends may be very crowded. There are playgrounds, picnic and camping facilities, an 18-hole golf course, boat docks, a snack shop, and a restaurant. In winter, skis, sleds, and toboggans are available for rent. River Lea, once the summer home of Grover Cleveland (the second mayor of Buffalo to become president), is in the park and now restored as a museum.

Take Route 190 to Grand Island and take exit 18b (the second one from the South Grand Island bridges). Follow the signs to the park entrance. Admission fee.

Buckhorn State Park: This 896-acre park is the very opposite of Beaver Island. It is at the north end of Grand Island and is undeveloped, apart from a small road in and a parking area. It contains a 250-acre wetland—open water and marsh adjacent to two streams: Burnt Ship Creek and Woods Creek. There are also trails through an upland forest of oak, hickory, and ash.

In early spring, when we were there, the trails were still snow-covered and tracked by cross-country skis. Red-wing blackbirds were hanging from the reeds, trilling; skunk cabbage was unfurling along the marsh edge. Great blue heron and other waterfowl frequent the marsh. There is no fee.

Take Route 190 to exit 20a (West River Road). Head east for about 1½ miles to the park entrance on your left. A dirt road leads into a parking area and trails.

Isle View, Niawanda, Fisherman's, Veteran's parks: All along the Niagara River, stretching north through the Tonawandas, are thin strips of parks for boat-launching and picnicking. Isle View (facing Grand Island) has the added attractions of an observation tower and Veteran's Park across the road, where there are playgrounds. Twomile Creek separates Isle View from Niawanda Park to the north. Take Niagara Street/River Road north from Buffalo along the river. If you are biking, take Riverwalk.

Ellicott Creek Park, at Niagara Falls Boulevard and South Creek Road, is a 165-acre children's paradise of swings, slides, jungle gyms—all spaced well apart so that no one section is particularly crowded. There are ball fields, tennis courts, stone picnic pavilions (built by WPA craftsmen), and a good winter sledding hill. The low cleared swath of land near the park entrance at Niagara Falls Boulevard provides a spillway from Ellicott Creek to Tonawanda Creek, a half mile to the north. A pleasant journey to the park is on the Ellicott Creek Bicycle Path. (See "Bicycle and Pedestrian Pathways," p. 29.)

Ellicott Creek Park is also a good place to put in a canoe or kayak and paddle upstream or down along the gently flowing creek. You may see snapping turtles, woodchucks, and, more unusually, the green heron, which seems to be this creek's totemic bird. Tucked down between the quiet creekbanks, you will hardly believe how close you glide to shopping malls and busy highways.

Ellicott Creek Island Park is a separate part of the park, not on Ellicott Creek but on Tonawanda Creek. Created when a new channel was dug to straighten the

Barge Canal, this quiet, secluded, carless island is now a pretty grove, dotted with small pavilions and a few swings and slides—a nice place to picnic.

Turn west off Niagara Falls Boulevard at Creekside Drive and park in the area immediately to your right. Take the footbridge over to the island.

Tonawanda Farmers' Market is the place to go on Saturday morning if you want fresh local produce at reasonable prices. You also find varieties here that the supermarkets have never heard of (and once you have eaten Silver Queen corn-on-the-cob or Irondequoit cantelope, the other kinds will never taste so sweet). To

get to the Tonawanda market, take Colvin Boulevard to Robinson Road. Turn west on Robinson. The market is a few blocks down on the right.

Buffalo has two farmers' markets: one at Bailey and Clinton Streets, the other at 999 Broadway. A variety of ethnic food shops inside the Broadway Market give it a unique old-world atmosphere.

AMHERST, WILLIAMSVILLE, & CHEEKTOWAGA

Glen Park, in the Village of Williamsville at Main and Mill Streets, centers on the picturesque waterfall where Ellicott Creek crosses the Onondaga Escarpment. This is a fine place for a winter walk because it is easily accessible, and a lovely stretch of woods following the creek downstream from Glen Avenue offers protection from the wind. In summer, it is fun to explore the paths along the banks and to wade in the shallow riffling creek. The Williamsville Water Mill, built in 1811, is on the south side of the creek at Main Street and offers fresh pressed cider in the fall. The park continues on the east side of Main, on an island in Ellicott Creek accessed by a footbridge. Here are picnic areas and plenty of mallard ducks.

Great Baehr Swamp is a large conservation area in the center of the Town of Amherst. One of the best remaining examples of swamp forest in Erie County, most of the almost 500-acre area has been acquired locally and through state funds and is maintained by the town for its open space, wildlife, and flood storage values. It contains 48-acre Margaret Louise Park, which has trails, picnic pagodas, restrooms, and a lookout platform and ramp for handicapped access. Some trails have been cleared through the rest of the swamp also. Great Baehr Swamp takes its name from the original owner who farmed the land.

    Take Maple Road to Hopkins. Head north on Hopkins for about three miles. The swamp is on both sides of the road. The park and parking area are on the left (west) side of Hopkins.

Reinstein Woods State Nature Preserve: In the midst of Cheektowaga, this 280-acre nature preserve contains a

unique 80-acre virgin forest of old-growth cherry, sugar maple, and beech trees. Its many ponds form the headwaters of Slate Bottom Creek (tributary to Cayuga Creek and thence, Buffalo River). Beaver, deer, mink, turtles, great blue heron, ducks, and other waterfowl all live here.

We owe the preserve to Dr. Victor Reinstein who acquired the land before it was developed, recognizing its natural beauty and value as habitat. He laid out a system of trails, built a retreat that now functions as a visitors' center, and devoted the latter part of his life to ensuring that the place remain forever wild. He finally arranged for New York State to takeover the site; a trust fund provides for a manager and for continued maintenance.

The preserve is visitable by reservation only. You can schedule an individual or group visit on most Wednesday or Saturday mornings, from spring through fall. Once there, you will follow the preserve manager's guided tour, which takes about two hours. Reinstein Preserve's value is enhanced by its adjacency to 200-acre Stiglemeier Park, owned by the Town of Cheektowaga.

Take Route 90 to the Walden Avenue east exit, and Walden Avenue to Union Road (Route 277). Turn right (south) on Union and continue one mile to Como Park Boulevard. Turn left (east) onto Como Park and continue for about 1½ miles. You will see the Reinstein Preserve sign on your right. A right on Honorine Drive brings you to the preserve entrance.

HAMBURG & ORCHARD PARK

Smoke's Creek is another largely neglected creek with hidden treasures. It is named after "Old Smoke" or "Old King," chief sachem of the Seneca at Kanesadaga (Geneva) until Sullivan's raid in 1779. According to Ketchum's *History of Buffalo,* Old Smoke's son, "Young King, held the important office of internuncius between the grand council of the Six Nations and the Seneca Nation. He bore the smoking brand from the great fire to kindle that of the Senecas. His official name was Gui-yah-gwaah-doh, meaning 'the smoke has passed.' " Old Smoke died and was buried at Smoke's Creek.

Upstream, in the Town of Hamburg, Smoke's Creek winds through a park and offers good fossil hunting. In the bedrock shales of the Moscow Formation (Middle Devonian), there are trilobite beds (on the left bank, past the prominent talus on the right) and, further upstream where the creek makes a hairpin turn, many brachiopods. The science museum geologists sometimes lead field trips here.

Take Route 90 west to Route 219 and the Mile Strip Road exit. Head east on Mile Strip about one mile to Abbott Road. Turn left. Park at the fire station, cross the footbridge, and climb the bank to the park. Follow the creek path upstream, beyond the park, and through the woods to where the banks are accessible. You will see signs of digging in several places along the creek bed.

Eighteenmile Creek begins just south of Boston, flows north to the Village of Hamburg, and then west through a beautiful meandering gorge to Lake Erie. The gorge is a classic fossil-collecting site. Access to it is provided by bridges where Route 20, Route 5, and Old Lake Shore Road cross the creek. From the bridge on Old Lake Shore Road you can walk downstream to the creek's mouth, a favorite fishing spot. There the bluffs are among the highest along Lake Erie's shore, exposing over 100 feet of Middle and Late Devonian rock strata. The crinoid-packed Tichenor Limestone, a thick ledge between the fossiliferous upper Hamilton shales, stands out prominently halfway up the cliff. Brachiopods, corals, crinoids, and trilobites from this and the overlying Genesee formation litter the beach.

There is a 464-acre undeveloped county park where the south branch and the main creek join. The gorge here is 60 feet deep. Pelecypods are commonly found in the

Tichenor Limestone here and brachiopods, crinoids, corals, and trilobites in the overlying shales. Septarium concretions, sometimes mistaken for fossilized turtles, may be seen in the gorge walls along the creek.

There are many informal approaches to Eighteenmile. Here are a few:

• To get to the county park area, take Route 20 to North Creek Road. Head east on North Creek for a total of about 1½ miles. About a half mile past Heltz Road, North Creek Road curves sharply to the left. The gorge walls here are sheer and steep. There is a wide shoulder on the left for parking. Across the road, follow the guardrail almost to the end (east end) until you come to a trail that winds you safely down.

• Another beautiful part of the gorge can be reached where Route 20 crosses it. Turn east on South Creek Road and park by the cemetery. You will see an old dirt road leading down to the creek.

• For dramatic overviews of the gorge, take Old Lakeview Road, which branches off from Lakeview Road just west of the Village of Hamburg.

Chestnut Ridge Park: This 1,213-acre park for all seasons, just 14 miles south of

Buffalo, is especially convenient to city residents in winter. The eastern section (the park is bisected by Route 277) is visually dominated by a large hillside—part of the Portage Escarpment, where the Allegheny Plateau meets the Erie Plain. Here are toboggan slides, a ski slope (with tow), cross-country trails, and great views of

downtown Buffalo, Lackawanna, and Lake Erie to the north. There is also a casino where you can thaw out with hot cocoa and food from the grill.

In the western section of the park you will find plenty of private, rustic picnic areas, open playgrounds, and woodland trails. Some 90 acres of this area is within the Shale Creek Nature Area, operated by the Buffalo Museum of Science. Neuman Creek and its high-walled tributaries crisscross the park.

Take Route 219 south from Buffalo to the Duell's Corner exit (east), which brings you to Route 277 (Chestnut Ridge Road). Continue on 277 south about two miles to the park entrance.

EVANS, BRANT/SOUTH LAKE ERIE SHORE

Sturgeon Point is a 200-slip marina in North Evans, 20 miles southwest of downtown Buffalo. It is also a favorite fishing area; the Department of Environmental Conservation releases Coho salmon and brown trout fingerlings here. There are washrooms, a snackbar, and a picnic area.

Take Route 5 west to Sturgeon Point Road, where you turn right. The Marina is at the end of the road.

Wendt Beach: This 178-acre county park, 22 miles southwest of Buffalo, has a lifeguarded swimming beach with a playground and shady picnic spots, wash-rooms, and a snack bar. No fee. The old Wendt mansion overlooks Lake Erie. Its main floor is open by reservation to non-profit social groups.

Take Route 5 west to Sturgeon Point Road and turn right. Proceed to Old Lake Shore Road where you turn left. Wendt Beach is on the right.

Bennett Beach, at the mouth of Big Sister Creek, just west of the Village of Angola, is one of the nicer beaches in the area. Large old willows shade a parking lot and picnic area. A walk across a foot-bridge over the creek brings you to the beach, which is lifeguarded. Sailboats harbor in the mouth of the creek. A natural sandbar forms some 50 feet out from the shore, making the underwater portion of the beach very sandy. The beach dunes here (the only ones remaining in Erie County) are eroding, but residents have begun to plant some dune areas in an effort to stabilize them. Bennett Beach is about 23 miles from Buffalo.

Take Route 5 west to Bennett Road, just outside the Village of Angola, and turn west. Bennett Road follows Big Sister Creek to the lake and park entrance.

Evangola State Park: Twenty-five miles southwest of Buffalo, this 733-acre park is noted for its 4,000-foot-long, clean sandy beach. Alert beachcombers may find interesting fossils that have weathered out of the shale cliffs nearby. The beach is lifeguarded with bathhouses, picnic and play areas, and a snack bar.

There are 80 campsites (12 with electricity hook-ups) and shower and laundry facilities. Campsite fee: $10.00 per day; $2.00 extra for electric. Reservations can be made from 90 to 7 days in advance of your arrival, or you can just show up and hope there is room. For reservations, call 1–800–456–CAMP.

Take Route 5 southwest to the park entrance. ■

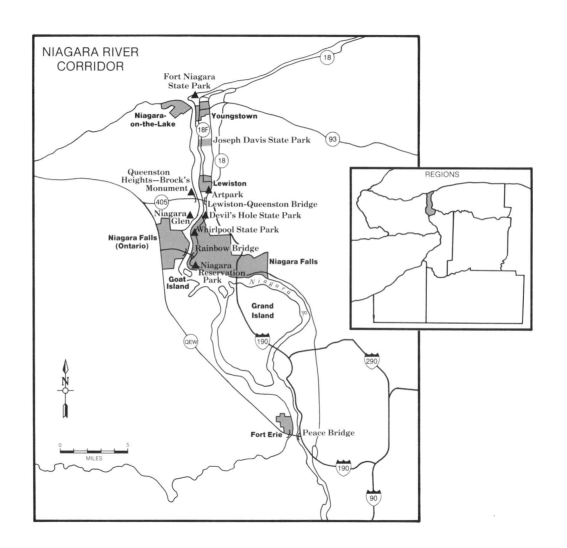

NIAGARA RIVER
CORRIDOR

Fort Niagara
State Park

Niagara-
on-the-Lake

Youngstown

18F

Joseph Davis State Park

18

Queenston
Heights—Brock's
Monument

Lewiston

Artpark

405

Lewiston-Queenston Bridge

Niagara
Glen

Devil's Hole State Park

Whirlpool State Park

Niagara Falls
(Ontario)

Rainbow Bridge

Niagara Falls

Niagara
Reservation
Park

Goat
Island

Niagara R.

Grand
Island

QEW

190

290

N

190

MILES

0   5

Fort Erie

Peace Bridge

190

90

18

93

REGIONS

SECTION

NIAGARA RIVER CORRIDOR

Betwixt the Lake Ontario and Erie, there is a vast and prodigious Cadence of Water which falls down after a surprizing and astonishing manner, insomuch that the Universe does not afford its Parallel. . . . At the foot of this horrible Precipice, we meet with the River Niagara, which is not above a quarter League broad, but is wonderfully deep in some places. It is so rapid above this Descent, that it violently hurries down the wild Beasts while endeavouring to pass it to feed on the other side, they not being able to withstand the force of its Current, which inevitably casts them headlong above Six hundred foot high.

This wonderful Downfal, is compounded of two great Cross-streams of Water, and two Falls, with an Isle sloping along the middle of it. The Waters which fall from this horrible Precipice do foam and boyl after the most hideous manner imaginable, making an outrageous Noise, more terrible than that of Thunder; for when the Wind blows out of the South, their dismal roaring may be heard more then Fifteen Leagues off. (First written description of Niagara Falls, Father Hennepin, *A New Discovery of a Vast Country in America*, 1698)

I shall Ladies and Gentlemen, on Saturday next, Oct. 17th, precisely at 3 o'clock, P.M. LEAP at the FALLS of NIAGARA, from a height of 120 to 130 feet, (being 40 to 50 feet higher than I leapt before,) into the eddy below. On my way down from Buffalo, on the morning of that day, in the Steamboat Niagara, I shall, for the amusement of the Ladies, doff my coat and spring from the mast head into the Niagara River. (Sam Patch, of Passaic Falls, New Jersey, from the *Colonial Advocate*, October 15, 1829)

"Les Chutes du Niagara Falls," painting by H. Sebron, 1852.

The compelling power of Niagara Falls is readily felt when you stand at the brink, but difficult to convey in plain words. Writers on the subject, including Father Hennepin, have been guilty of the greatest exaggerations in their attempts to sufficiently impress their readers. Stunters walked, rolled, and carried each other across the gorge on tightropes or tumbled over the cataract in barrels—the success of these feats depending on our intuitive sense of the force they defied. On October 17, 1829, Sam Patch catapulted himself to national fame when he jumped into the falls from a platform at the brink of Goat Island, and then climbed, without a scratch, from the rocks below.

Without embellishment, the Niagara *is* probably the most powerfully situated river in the country. It is the Great Lakes connection to the sea. It is a border between two nations and a historic battleground. It drives the largest hydroelectric development in the Western world. And near its heart lies the honeymoon capital of the world, Niagara Falls, which attracts some five million people every year.

Niagara Falls. (Courtesy Buffalo and Erie County Historical Society)

NIAGARA FALLS: CANADIAN SIDE

Niagara Parkway: The prettiest way to approach the falls from Buffalo is on the Niagara Parkway, which runs hard by the river (Canadian side) all the way from Fort Erie to Niagara-on-the-Lake. Cross the Peace Bridge, and two sharp right turns past Canadian customs bring you to the town of Fort Erie and the Niagara Parkway. (If you are in a hurry, however, take Route 190 across Grand Island to the Robert Moses Parkway. You can cross into Canada just below the falls at the Rainbow Bridge.)

The Niagara Parkway is a pleasant place to hike, bicycle, or have a picnic. There are paths, picnic areas, and historical markers all along the river. The Upper Niagara Marina, two miles downriver from Fort Erie, has boat services. Swim-

ming is possible at the public beach in Fort Erie, at Kings Bridge Park in the town of Chippawa, or at Dufferin Islands, a provincial park about a half mile before the falls. A chain of canals channeled from the Niagara River forms the islands, which are connected by a maze of paths and footbridges, offering many lovely private places to picnic. There is also a central lifeguarded beach here with a bathhouse, washrooms, a concession stand, and paddle boats. No fee.

Queen Victoria Park, extending along the Niagara Parkway from **Dufferin Islands** to the Rainbow Bridge, gives you the Canadian (Horseshoe) falls, but is also worth looking at itself. There are year-round flower displays in the park's greenhouse across the parkway from the falls, as well as pleasant places for tea or lunch nearby. Extensive outdoor gardens include Oakes Garden Theater, near the Rainbow Bridge, which has lily ponds, promenades, and a Greek-style amphitheater.

In summer this strip of the Niagara Parkway sees heavy traffic. If approaching from the south, park above the falls and walk to them. It is also much more dra-

matic to come upon them this way. Table Rock House, at the brink of the Horseshoe Falls, is the entrance to the Table Rock Scenic Tunnel, which you reach (after paying admission) by taking an elevator down through 125 feet of solid rock. The tunnel leads to an observation plat-

form below the Horseshoe Falls and to viewing portals behind them. Table Rock House has snack and souvenir shops, washrooms, and a picnic area outside.

If you want to take one of the *Maid of the Mist* boats, which pass directly in front of the falls, use the incline railway just south of the Rainbow Bridge to reach the boarding platform. There is a fee.

For panoramic views of the falls there are three towers: the 325-foot observation tower at the Panasonic Center, which is closest to the Horseshoe Falls, the 800-foot Skylon Tower, and the 350-foot Canada Tower near the entrance to the Rainbow Bridge. All charge admission.

NIAGARA FALLS: AMERICAN SIDE

Niagara Reservation Park includes all the land bordering the falls on the American side and Goat Island. Admission is free but there is a parking charge (good for one re-entry) for each of the three parking lots, two of which are on Goat Island.

Prospect Point, at the brink of the gorge, is the best place for a frontal view of the American falls. The 282-foot observation tower has stairways and elevators going up and down into the gorge, where you can board the *Maid of the Mist.* (The tower charges a small entry fee.) At 4:50 P.M., July 28, 1954, the old Prospect Point—185,000 tons of rock—dropped into the gorge. The base of the American falls is cluttered with rubble from this and several other rock falls.

Goat Island: You can drive, follow the footpaths, or take the Viewmobile train (in season) out to Goat Island, which divides the Canadian from the American falls (90 percent of the river's water goes over the Canadian Falls). Terrapin Point overlooks one cusp of the Canadian horseshoe; Luna Island, reached by footbridge, is on the verge of the Bridal Veil Falls, a part of the American falls. Even there, in mid-river, you can descend into the gorge for the Cave of the Winds trip, which takes you, by elevator, to a walkway at the base of the Bridal Veil Falls. Admission fee. (Waterproof clothing is provided.) Three Sisters Islands, joined by footbridges to the southern end of Goat Island, afford good viewing of the cascades above the falls.

There are two striking buildings near the entrance to the park. The admission-free **Wintergarden,** a glass-enclosed steel-frame greenhouse, connects, by climatized walkways, to the Hilton Hotel, the Convention Center, and Lackey Plaza, where there is an outdoor ice-skating rink (winter only) with skates available to rent. The **Native American Center for the Living Arts,** in the turtle-shaped building, features Iroquoian art, crafts, and foods, craft workshops, dance performances, and a variety of special events, including the dances and craft displays of visiting tribes from around the country. Open daily from 9 to 6. Admission fee. (716–284–2427)

The Schoellkopf Geological Museum has exhibits and a multiscreen theater presentation relating the geological history of the falls. Guides conduct walks along the gorge trails throughout the summer; in winter they organize cross-country ski tours through some of the parks nearby. The Upper Gorge Nature Trail begins behind the museum. Open seven days a week, from 10 to 5. From November 1 to Memorial Day, the museum is closed Mondays and Tuesdays. No fee. (716–278–1780)

From Niagara Reservation Park, take the Robert Moses Parkway north about a half mile to the museum, or walk the scenic path beginning at Prospect Point.

The Aquarium of Niagara Falls, the first major oceanarium in the United States to use synthetic seawater, has just about every kind of water animal—from barracuda, chambered nautilus, and trumpetfish to brittle stars. Dolphins, seals, and an electric eel perform hourly on weekends. There is something restful about the semi-dark, carpeted alcoves lined with green aquariums full of brilliantly colored fish. Even on crowded Sundays, visitors, including children, seem to relax and thoroughly enjoy themselves. The aquarium is connected by a pedestrian bridge to the geological museum (follow the directions above). Open from 9 to 5 every day except Thanksgiving, Christmas, and New Year's. Admission fee.

LOWER GORGE: CANADIAN SIDE

(continuing north on the Niagara Parkway)

The Whirlpool, 3½ miles below the falls, marks the place where the extinct St. David's River once entered this valley through a deep gorge similar to the Niagara's today. At the whirlpool the Niagara River has excavated debris from that ancient gorge and makes a deep right-angled bend in its course. Effects of the jet-stream current through the whirlpool can best be seen from Whirlpool State Park on the American side (see p. 46), or (for a fee) from the Whirlpool Aero Car, which crosses above it between two points on the Canadian side.

The Great Gorge Trip, a guided tour that begins just north of the Whirlpool Rapids Bridge, takes you by elevator down to a boardwalk that follows a narrow part of the gorge formed when the Niagara River drained only Lake Erie. Here the river drops 50 feet in less than a mile, creating terrific rapids. About 5,000 years ago, when the Upper Great Lakes began to flow past Detroit through Lake Erie, the Niagara River became a major erosive power, cutting the wide "Great Gorge" you see upstream all the way to the falls. The guide will explain all this and more. Admission fee.

Niagara Glen, located just below the whirlpool, is a good place for a family outing. Here the gorge is at its narrowest: 250 feet wide. Stairways and trails wind down from the brink of the gorge to the river's edge, providing a close look at geological formations along the way. When Niagara's falls reached this point, they were divided in two by a small island. The much larger eastern cataract eventually captured the headwaters of the western one, leaving its crest high and dry. Wintergreen Flats, now a picnic area, was the bed of this western branch. Giant potholes in rock debris near the river trail are the work of the old west falls. The park trail-guide identifies other formations and gives a brief geological history. Interesting plants, like the tuliptree and the sassafrass tree, grow in the protected moist atmosphere of the glen. You'll find a picnic shelter, a restaurant, washrooms, and several places along the river where fishing is allowed. No fee.

The Niagara Parks Commission School of Horticulture, just below Niagara Glen, is maintained by its gardening students, who also work in Ontario's other Niagara parks. Visitors are welcome to these studiously landscaped grounds; admission is free. A mile or so north, thousands of plants press together beneath the heavy (500 pounds each) hands of time to form the Floral Clock.

Queenston Heights: Brock's monument dominates this 100-acre park on the Niagara Escarpment. Sir Isaac Brock, whose remains are interred under the monument, was killed at Queenston by American forces in the War of 1812. Visitors can climb the circular steps to the top for a fine view of the Niagara Peninsula clear north to Toronto. Sunday afternoon concerts take place in the park throughout the summer. There are concession stands, washrooms, and a restaurant with indoor and outdoor seating and great views of the gorge and points north. No park fee.

The 480-mile-long Bruce Trail begins at Queenston Heights and continues to Tobermory, on the Bruce Peninsula at Georgian Bay.

Niagara-on-the-Lake, at the mouth of the river on Lake Ontario, looks like a 19th-century village. Galleries, restaurants, and giftshops are mostly housed in restored century-old buildings along quiet, shaded streets. There is a pretty park at the town's

center with a playground, a pool, and picnic facilities. Located in and around town are the Niagara Historical Museum, the Shaw Festival Theater, and Fort George, a British post on the frontier from 1796 to 1813, when the Americans temporarily captured it. It has been restored and is open to tourists. Admission fee.

LOWER GORGE: AMERICAN SIDE

(continuing north on the Robert Moses Parkway)

Whirlpool State Park provides excellent views of the river's 90-degree turn at the whirlpool, 3½ miles below the falls. From the parking lot, the gorge-rim path leads to a stone stairway down to the river. At Whirlpool Point you can see the jet stream entering the pool and, between 8 and 9 A.M. daily in the summer, the reversal of current through the whirlpool caused by the sudden increase in waterflow over the falls. (During viewing hours the hydroelectric plants allow the flow to increase from 50,000 cubic feet per second to at least 100,000 cfs.) Follow the river path upstream for about a mile to see the Whirlpool Rapids, and then retrace your steps for the climb back up (round trip: 3¼ miles) or continue downstream on a trail that leads to Devil's Hole. No fee.

Devil's Hole State Park (parking lot, 1½ miles north of Whirlpool State Park) is the scene of a 1763 massacre in which a party of British soldiers hauling goods over the Portage Trail were pushed into the gulch by a Seneca war party. Devil's Hole also marks the end of one of the channels that drained Lake Tonawanda several thousand years ago. The main trail leads down in a spectacular series of switchbacks to the embankment of the Old Niagara Gorge Railroad, about 25 feet above the river. Look for a wide-mouthed, 50-foot-long cave near the bottom of the gorge—in legend, the home of the evil spirit, which gives the place its name. Take the side trail that leads north to the Power House or continue south on the main trail past the Rock of Ages (a two-story-high point of limestone that fell from the wall above) to the steep switchback trail leading to the rim, one mile south of where you began. Return on the rim trail (round trip: 2.7 miles). No fee.

The Power Vista: This visitors' center for the New York State Power Generating Plant is about a mile north of Devil's Hole. Its displays explain the power plant operation and describe the Niagara's history as a working river—beginning with the grist mills and paper mills that lined its banks in the 19th century. The Vista is another good spot for viewing the lower gorge. The main generating plant is below it and off limits to visitors. No fee.

Earl W. Brydges Artpark, at Lewiston, has become a major summer cultural center in New York State. Plays, concerts, classical ballet, modern dance, opera, and an annual jazz festival are presented in the 2,400-seat theater; outside, on the grounds and terraces, workshops, storytellings, and other forms of theater continually take place. Artpark's dramatic location—spanning the Niagara Escarpment—dictated the use of an extensive multilevel boardwalk to connect all the terraces and activity areas to the main theater. The site makes Artpark one of the best vantage

Artpark perfor-
mance artist

points on the gorge. From the upper terrace (park in the uppermost Portage Road lot), you can walk to a dirt haul road that rises gently along the gorge wall. The limestone and shale strata here are full of brachiopod and crinoid fossils. The road takes you back along the gorge as far as the Lewiston-Queenston Bridge, where there is a superb view of the Queenston Generating Station, which looks something like a giant cash register built into the opposite gorge wall. Following the ridge back (north) you will see, spread below you, the fan-shaped basin in which most of Lewiston lies. This was the original plunge basin of the infant Niagara, where it fell over the escarpment into glacial Lake Iroquois. Admission to Artpark is free, but there may be a parking charge in summer. For a program schedule call 716-754-9001.

Take Route 190 to Lewiston. A west turn off Center Street onto Fourth brings you to the main entrance.

Lewiston was once a strategic landing on the Atlantic-Mississippi waterway. Here goods were unpacked from boats coming up the Niagara River from Lake Ontario and transferred to carriers who hauled them up and over the escarpment and around the falls on the Portage Trail. Early on, the Seneca monopolized this porter business. The 1763 attack on British soldiers at Devil's Hole (see p. 46) was, in part, an effort to protect their monopoly.

Lewiston was burned to the ground in the War of 1812, but it was the completion of the Erie Canal in 1825 that ended its strategic importance. Today Lewiston is noted for its restaurants and its fine early 19th-century buildings. A pleasant walk begins at Artpark, takes you along the river (First and Water streets), and up Center Street, with its historic houses and tempting shops. The Lewiston Historical Museum (1833) is at Plain and Niagara streets.

Joseph Davis State Park, about two miles north of Lewiston, is a newly developed park whose main attraction is an Olympic-sized swimming pool. There are also a bath house, a wading pool, playgrounds, picnic facilities, and unmarked trails for cross-country skiing in winter. Admission fee.

From Lewiston take scenic Route 18F north to the park entrance sign.

Old Fort Niagara, Youngstown: At the mouth of the Niagara River overlooking Lake Ontario, Fort Niagara was occupied by either French, British, or American military forces from 1726, when LaSalle founded it, until the 1920s. During the summer, soldiers in period uniforms perform drills and fire a cannon. The buildings are open all year round. Admission fee.

The fort is within Fort Niagara State Park, which has picnic grounds, playing fields, swimming pools, and fishing and boat-launching areas. Admission fee. ■

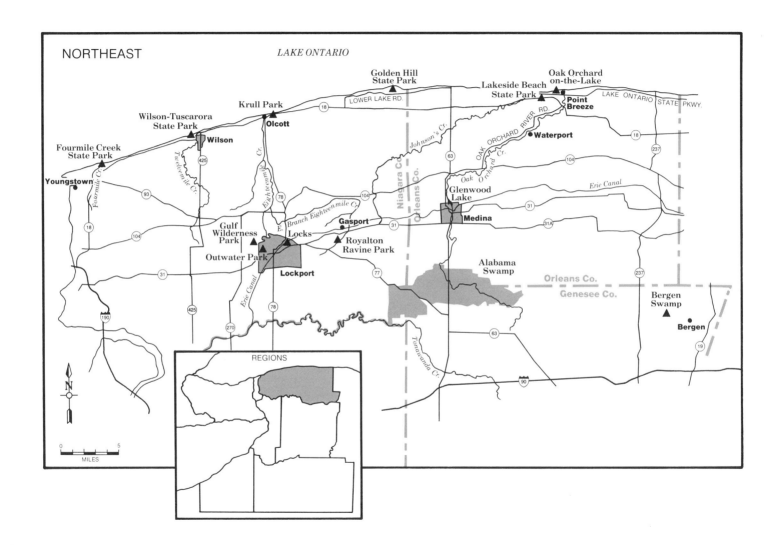

NORTHEAST

LAKE ONTARIO

Golden Hill State Park

Oak Orchard on-the-Lake

Lakeside Beach State Park

Point Breeze

LOWER LAKE RD.

LAKE ONTARIO STATE PKWY.

Krull Park

Olcott

Wilson-Tuscarora State Park

Wilson

OAK ORCHARD RIVER RD.

Waterport

Johnson's Cr.

Oak Orchard Cr.

Fourmile Creek State Park

Tuscarora Cr.

Youngstown

Fourmile Cr.

Eighteenmile Cr.

Oak Orchard Cr.

Erie Canal

Glenwood Lake

Niagara Co.

Orleans Co.

Medina

Branch Eighteenmile Cr.

Gasport

E. Locks

Gulf Wilderness Park

Royalton Ravine Park

Outwater Park

Lockport

Erie Canal

Alabama Swamp

Orleans Co.

Genesee Co.

Bergen Swamp

Bergen

Tonawanda Cr.

REGIONS

N

0   5

MILES

NORTHEAST

The cobblestone houses, orchards, and wetlands of the Ontario Plain are all, one way or another, legacies of Lake Ontario and its predecessor, glacial Lake Iroquois. Cobblestones as round as billiard balls were shaped by centuries of wave action and then deposited, along with tons of fieldstone, as Lake Iroquois receded. Thousands of years later farmers broke their backs clearing their land of this rubble.

Then, in the 1830s (or so the story goes), some resourceful out-of-work Erie Canal masons eyed the stone piles with sudden interest. They developed secret mortar formulas (each mason had his own) and designed a new kind of building in which rows of perfectly uniform cobblestones were set in angled layers of mortar over a rough-walled structure of fieldstone. The results were fairly indestructible, maintenance-free buildings with beautifully patterned surfaces of the blue, gray, pink, and mauve-toned stones that can be found all along Ontario's beaches.

To see some of the finest examples of this unique architecture (there are only about 600 cobblestone buildings in the United States, 500 of them in New York State), take Route 425 from Niagara Falls Boulevard in North Tonawanda about 20 miles north to Wilson, on the lakeshore. You will pass the cobblestone North Ridge Methodist Church (1848), at the junction of Route 425 and Route 93, and several cobblestone houses. The Wilson Historical Society (open Sundays 2 to 4) and the Country Barn Information Center can tell you about

tours. There are other cobblestone and fieldstone buildings along routes 18 and 104, including an old stage-coach inn on the latter at Oak Orchard on-the-Ridge.

As for orchards, they extend right across the Ontario Plain from the Niagara River to Oak Orchard Creek. Many varieties of apple (though not half as many as there used to be, old-timers will tell you), cherry, pear, peach, and plum trees shower

the roads with blossoms in spring. Along with the orchards, there are vineyards, cornfields, and pumpkin patches that yield rich harvests and fill the roadside stands in fall. Routes 104, 18, and 31 are all at their best at this time of the year.

ONTARIO LAKESHORE

Fourmile, Twelvemile, Eighteenmile, Johnson's, and Oak Orchard creeks, Lake Ontario's main tributaries in Niagara

and Orleans counties, are all good streams for fishing, although all the fish may not be safe to eat. (For fish advisory information, see Appendix.) Since the major lakeshore parks and harbors tend to be located at the creek mouths, we will describe particular boating and fishing opportunities park by park—heading east on Route 18 from Youngstown.

Fourmile Creek State Park is on the Robert Moses Parkway and state Route 18, three miles east of the Village of Youngstown. Like the other parks along Lake Ontario's south shore, it is mainly for fishing, picnicking, and camping (266 campsites, 102 with electricity), with no swimming and few playgrounds. Central shelters provide flush toilets, showers, and laundry facilities. The overnight camping fee is $10.00. Campsite reservations can be made in advance or when you arrive. For reservations: 1–800–456–CAMP.

Wilson-Tuscarora State Park, just west of Wilson at the mouth of Twelvemile Creek, offers good fishing and boating (with boat launches), as well as a transient marina at nearby Wilson Harbor. Boats

are available for rent here and at other marinas on the lake.

Krull Park: This 323-acre county park at Olcott (near the mouth of Eighteenmile Creek) is the nicest all-around family park along the south shore and the only one where swimming is permitted. Beautifully landscaped grounds with low stone walls, fine tall trees, and, in town, a small strip of amusement park with rides and arcades recall Olcott's prosperous days as a pleasure resort. Krull Park has baseball diamonds, tennis courts, horseshoe pits, plenty of playground equipment, a fishing pier, a small lifeguarded beach, and picnic facilities. No fee. Olcott Harbor is a nearby attraction.

Golden Hill State Park has 50 campsites (12 with electricity hook-ups), a boat

launch, and a 19th-century lighthouse. Its wooded grounds and stony beach are comparatively clean and quiet. To get here you have to turn off Route 18 about 10 miles east of Olcott onto Lovers' Lane, Johnson Creek, or Burgess Road to reach Lower Lake Road, then turn right.

Lakeside Beach State Park: This camping park (274 sites) has a slick, modern look that sharply contrasts with the other parks we've listed, perhaps due to the landscaping that accompanied the building of the Lake Ontario State Parkway, which extends west to the park. It offers the usual fare of campsites (all with electricity), picnic facilities, washrooms, and a stone beach. There is also a store and a laundry for campers' convenience. One natural extravagance in spring is the wildflower

population: the woods are carpeted with painted and purple trillium. The other attraction is nearby Point Breeze, where there is a marine park with boat launches and a breakwall from which to fish or birdwatch. Point Breeze is at the mouth of Oak Orchard Creek, a beautiful creek that deserves its own entry.

Oak Orchard Creek begins about 10 miles north of Batavia and meanders northward for some 70 miles to Lake Ontario, emptying at Point Breeze. The main artery of the Oak Orchard Wildlife Refuge, this creek is not only pretty but excellent for canoeing, fishing, and wildlife-watching.

Novice canoeists will enjoy the eight-mile section within the refuge; they can follow the slow-moving creek downstream from the Knowlesville Road bridge (at the Swallow Hollow parking area) to the Route 63 bridge (about three miles north of Alabama). For directions to these bridges, see "Alabama Swamp" (p. 58). Permission for this canoe trip is required from the Refuge Headquarters (Casey Road) in order to protect waterfowl nesting areas. Stop in or write: Iroquois National Wildlife Refuge Headquarters, Basom, N.Y. 10403.

Experienced canoeists can take the section of the creek beginning about two miles north of Medina (at the West Scott/Slade Road bridge) and continuing for 12 to 15 miles north. There are several sections of white water and places where you may have to thread your way through fallen trees. About three miles before Kenyonville, Oak Orchard Creek broadens into Lake Alice and is open to fast traffic—motor boats, water skiers, etc. You can get out at the low Kenyonville Road bridge (on the right side of the creek, just beyond the bridge) or continue on another three miles to the Route 279 bridge at Waterport.

To get to the starting point for this canoe trip, take Route 63 north, from the Village of Alabama, through Medina. Two miles past Medina turn right onto West Scott/Slade Road. The creek is just ahead. Put in on the left side of the road.

Fishermen tend to concentrate at the creek mouth or at the Waterport dam. Coho salmon and lake trout are the specialties here. If you're just looking for a pleasant drive, take Route 104 (Ridge Road) east to Oak Orchard on-the-Ridge, and

turn left at the cobblestone stage-coach inn onto Oak Orchard River Road, which follows the creek to Lake Ontario. This drive is especially rewarding in late spring. While the rest of the countryside still seems shut down for the winter, and Lake Ontario looks as bleak as the Baltic, Oak Orchard Creek sports canoes and early-blossoming orchards all along its banks.

LOCKPORT

The city of Lockport is known to visitors mainly for the Erie Canal locks at its center. But there are other points of real interest: notably, a magnificent view from atop the Niagara Escarpment at Outwater Park, a wildflower-lover's paradise in Gulf Wilderness Park, and a range of 19th-century architecture from mill ruins in Lowertown to the many well preserved Victorian houses in the city's southeast quarter.

Take Route 78 (Transit Road) north from Buffalo.

Erie Canal: The most difficult section of the Erie Canal to construct was where it crossed the Niagara Escarpment in Lock-

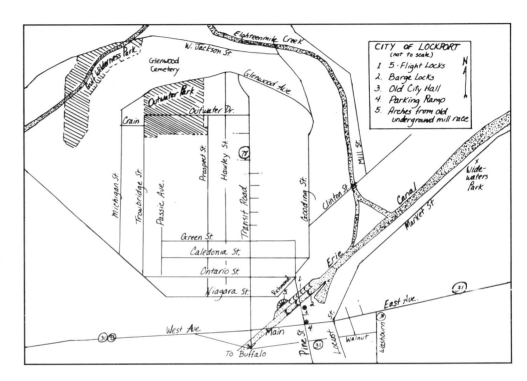

port. A deep cut for the original twin set of five-flight locks had to be blasted out of the Lockport Dolomite caprock so that canal boats could climb over the ridge—or, as the ad read, "sail uphill through Clinton's Ditch." Only one set of the old locks remains; it can be seen from the Pine

Street Bridge. A walkway from Pine Street takes you down alongside the two barge locks that replaced the old locks in 1918 and are still used by pleasure craft on the canal. From Memorial Day to Labor Day these boats pass through, some on their way from the Caribbean via the Intercoastal Waterway, Hudson River, Erie Canal, and Niagara River to eventually berth in the Upper Great Lakes.

Narrated boat tours of the Lockport locks and Erie Barge Canal depart from Widewaters Marina, on Market Street in Lockport. These are offered afternoons, Wednesday through Sunday, from May through November. Lunch and dinner tours and special group tours are available. For information or reservations call: 716-693-3260.

If you prefer to walk, take the Canal Trail, which follows the old towpath once used by the horses and mules that pulled the barges. The trail runs from Lockport through Gasport to Genesee Valley Park, south of Rochester. Walkers, bicyclists, or cross-country skiers can pick it up at Widewaters Park and travel east past apple orchards,

woodlands, and many fine old buildings made of Lockport Dolomite.

Among the many architecturally interesting buildings in Lockport are the old city hall, originally a flour mill, now a friendly bar and restaurant on Pine Street; the Niagara County Court House on Niagara Street; and the Farmers' and Mechanics' Bank building, a tall landmark on the corner of Main and Locust streets.

Along Clinton, Gooding, and Mill streets you will see many old industrial buildings and mill ruins. And along all the streets in the southeast quarter there are fine century-old houses, including the Kenan Center, at 433 Locust Street, which now houses arts-and-crafts exhibits and theater productions. In winter there is an indoor skating rink. Admission fee varies.

The Niagara County Historical Mu-

seum, at Niagara and Prospect Streets, has restored Victorian rooms, canal displays, photographs, and memorabilia of early Niagara County settlers. Open Thursday through Sunday from 1 to 5 P.M. There is no fee.

Outwater Park: For breathtaking views from the Niagara Escarpment, we suggest the following approach:

Take Route 78 north through Lockport *past* Outwater Drive (east entrance to the park) to Glenwood Avenue. Turn left. As you head west on Glenwood, the eroding wall of the escarpment is on the left, and a spectacular view of the Ontario Plain and Lake Ontario, 10 miles north, opens above Glenwood Cemetery to the right. Glenwood Avenue brings you to Crain Street. Turn left to reach the west side of Outwater Park (jog left at the end of Crain to reach Outwater Drive). Outwater Drive brings you to another fine overlook from which, on a clear day, you can see north as far as Toronto.

This high ridge diverted Lake Tonawanda spillways west, creating the Lockport Gulf, and east, cutting the gap in the escarpment later utilized by the Erie

Canal. Samuel Outwater, who donated the park to the city, could not have given it a more fitting name.

This 47½-acre park has tennis, basketball, horseshoe, and lawn bowling courts, baseball diamonds, swimming pools, playgrounds, picnic groves, and washrooms. There is a snack shop open in summer. No fee.

Rollin T. Grant Gulf Wilderness Park: Glacial Lake Tonawanda, draining westward over the escarpment, cut this gulf, which is now used by Eighteenmile Creek. Several trails loop through the climax forest along both sides of the creek, passing a falls, a mineral spring, and a small pond. Among the many spring wildflowers we saw were bloodroot, false and true soloman's seal, wild ginger, toothwort, adder's tongue, trillium, and troutlily. The Buffalo Museum of Science sometimes schedules wildflower identification walks to this 75-acre park. There are no facilities—and no fee.

Take Route 78 north through Lockport to Caledonia Street and turn right to reach Gooding Street. Turn left (north) on Gooding to reach West Jackson Street. Follow West Jackson west about 1½ miles to the park entrance on the left. Park on the road. West Jackson Street is interesting in itself. It follows the creek through the gulf cut by Lake Tonawanda spillwaters, where a lower raw face of the Niagara Escarpment is exposed. The red Grimsby Sandstone you see here was deposited some 430 million years ago in the Early Silurian Period.

Rollin T. Grant, by the way, was not so very long ago a mayor of Lockport.

Royalton Ravine, just south of the Village of Gasport, is the remnant of yet another spillway of glacial Lake Tonawanda over the Niagara Escarpment. Now it is home to the east branch of Eighteenmile Creek and a 156-acre county park, the Victor M. Fitchee Royalton Ravine Conservation Education Center, which is dedicated to its preservation as a natural area.

A trail leads to the bottom of the ravine where a 150-foot-long wooden swinging footbridge crosses the creek. This is a great attraction to kids of all ages. From here, the trail climbs to a clearing where you will see the ruins of an old homestead. A short trail on the right, past the old house, takes you to Royalton Falls.

Take Transit Road (Route 78) to Route 31 in Lockport. Head east on Route 31 to Route 77. Turn right on 77 and continue to Gasport Road where you turn left (north). Royalton Ravine Park is on your left, a short way after you pass Mill Road.

NORTHERN GENESEE COUNTY

Alabama Swamp: From early March through April, the Canada geese return north after wintering along Delaware and Chesapeake bays. They stop, along with mallards, black ducks, pin-tails, blue- and green-winged teal, wood ducks, shovellers, gadwalls, and whistling swans, in the "Alabama Swamp"—20,000 acres of prime

waterfowl habitat located midway between Buffalo and Rochester on the Atlantic flyway. Officially, the central 10,818 acres of this marshland are the Iroquois National Wildlife Refuge. It is flanked by state wildlife management areas: Tonawanda to the west, Oak Orchard to the east. All three sections have interpretive trails, overlooks, and photography blinds for viewing wildlife. Canoeing and fishing are permitted on certain parts of Oak Orchard Creek— check with refuge headquarters on Casey Road for details. (Also see "Oak Orchard Creek" on page 54.) State-managed areas permit hunting and trapping, in season.

This once extensive marshland, descended from glacial Lake Tonawanda, was endangered by the drainage schemes of farmers and developers until about 20 years ago, when wildlife services began to preserve and restore the wetlands. Now dikes contain the creek flood-waters, creating shallow paddies, which are planted with buckwheat and millet to provide browsing for the migrant birds. Nesting flocks of ducks and geese have established in the refuge, and species long vanished from this area, like the bald eagle, have recently been reintroduced.

In mid-April, the Canada goose migration peaks; an average of 40,000 are in and around the refuge at this time. By mid-May they are gone to nesting grounds in northern Canada. Fall migration through the swamp is much smaller (peaking at about 5,000) because the geese tend to pass east of the area. Like the geese, people are drawn to Alabama Swamp in spring and fall. Remember though that the trails are most accessible in winter (with snowshoes or cross-country skis) and in summer, when the woodbine, wild grape, and waterlilies are in full leaf.

Take the Thruway east to the Pembroke exit (48A). Go north on Route 77/63 past the Tonawanda Indian Reservation and past the state game farm to Alabama, where 77 and 63 part ways. (The Alabama Hotel on the corner serves a good old-fashioned Sunday dinner.) Continue north to Casey Road (left) where you'll find the refuge headquarters open from 9 to 4, Monday through Friday, all year round, and on weekends during spring and fall migrations. They have maps, trail guides, displays, and films about waterfowl. To reach the Swallow Hollow boardwalk trail, turn east on Lewiston Road (back at the hotel) and, after about two miles, north on Knowlesville Road. After it veers right, follow this road for about two more miles across the bridge over Oak Orchard Creek to a parking area on the left. In spring the maples along this route are tapped, and you can buy fresh maple syrup from the sugarhouse. Route 77 west from the hotel takes you through the Tonawanda Creek area. There are two wetland overlooks along the road where many geese and other waterfowl may be seen if the time is right (dawn and dusk are usually best). It is 12 miles via routes 77 and 31 to Lockport, where you can pick up Route 78 south to Buffalo.

Bergen Swamp: Owned by the Bergen Swamp Preservation Society, the unique environment here is actually a marl bog. Marl bogs develop over limestone and support many plants that cannot grow in more acidic bogs. Liverwort, mosses, horsetails, ferns, and ground pine grow here along with rarer species like the carniverous pitcher plant and the showy lady's slipper orchid. Migrating birds, including many species of warbler, use the area. The swamp is open to the public (day trips only), but the society recommends guided tours because the trails are not marked and it is easy to get lost. The pygmy rattlesnake, another rarity in Western New York, does live in the swamp and presents a possible hazard.

For further information write to the Bergen Swamp Preservation Society, Inc., c/o Rochester Museum of Arts and Science, 657 East Avenue, Rochester, N.Y. 14607.

Take Route 90 east to exit 47 and Route 19 north to Bergen. Continue north on Route 19 after it becomes Lake Road for about two blocks to Hunter Street. Turn left on Hunter Street, which becomes Swamp Road. Take Swamp Road to Hessenthaler Road (about 3½ miles from Bergen) and turn right. Park on the road and walk to the marked trail that leads to the swamp. ■

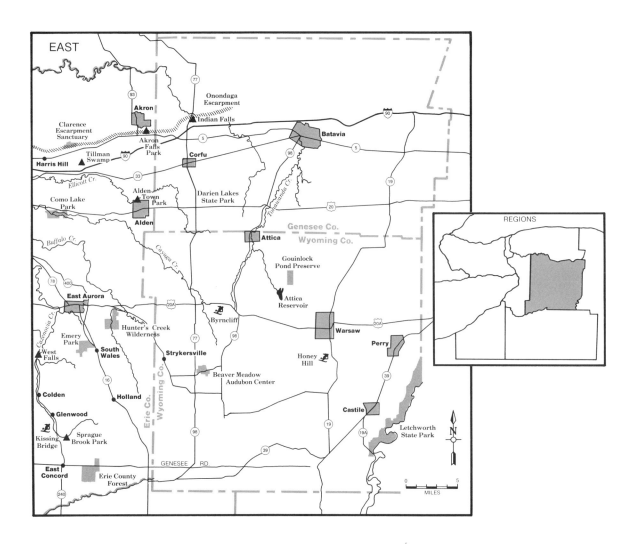

EAST

Onondaga Escarpment

93
77

Akron

Clarence Escarpment Sanctuary

Indian Falls

Batavia

90

Akron Falls Park

5

Corfu

5

Tillman Swamp

90

Harris Hill

98

19

33

Ellicott Cr.

Alden Town Park

Darien Lakes State Park

Como Lake Park

Alden

Tonawanda Cr.

20

Buffalo Cr.

Genesee Co.

Attica

Wyoming Co.

Coyuga Cr.

Gouinlock Pond Preserve

78
400

East Aurora

Attica Reservoir

Cazenovia Cr.

20A

Hunter's Creek Wilderness

Byrncliff

Warsaw

20A

Emery Park

77

98

Perry

West Falls

South Wales

Strykersville

Honey Hill

Erie Co.

Wyoming Co.

16

Colden

Holland

Beaver Meadow Audubon Center

39

Glenwood

98

Castile

Kissing Bridge

Sprague Brook Park

19

Letchworth State Park

19A

N

East Concord

Erie County Forest

39

GENESEE RD.

240

0   5
MILES

REGIONS

SECTION

EAST

EASTERN ERIE COUNTY

Clarence Escarpment Sanctuary:

Owned by the Nature Conservancy, this 27-acre sanctuary preserves a section of the Onondaga Escarpment, the 30- to 70-foot-high bluff that extends across Western New York from Buffalo. (For more on the significance of this distinct geographic feature, see Section 1.)

The Escarpment Sanctuary is rich in geological and botanical features. The escarpment is 375 to 410 million years old; the limes, muds, and silicas were deposited during the Late Silurian and Middle Devonian periods. Of interest to geologists is the un-conformity, or time gap, about one-third of the way down the ledge face, between the Edgecliff Member (Middle Devonian) and the underlying 10-foot section of light Akron Dolostone (Late Silurian). Most of the Early Devonian sediments and rocks were eroded away before the Edgecliff limestone was deposited. This unconformity is the only one in Erie County and can be traced for over 1,000 feet along the ledge face. Beneath is the Bertie Formation, in which the fossil eurypterid is found.

The moist shaded calcareous environment provided by the escarpment is suited to many unusual calciphilic plants now absent in much of New York State such as bladder fern, maidenhair spleenwort, and rock tripe liverwort.

Take the Thruway (Route 90) to exit 49 (Depew/Transit Road). Head north on Transit (Route 78) about one mile to Main Street (Route 5). Turn right (east) and drive about three miles to Goodrich Road. Proceed north on Goodrich to the first crossroad, Greiner Road. Turn east (right) on Greiner and continue a quarter of a mile to the Sanctuary parking lot on your right. Near the "Clarence Sanctuary" sign, you will see an informal path that leads you to a pond

at the base of the escarpment, across it on a broken-down foot-bridge, and up through the woods along the escarpment ridge.

Tillman Road Swamp Wildlife Management Area:

This 230-acre state-managed land includes about 80 acres of emergent freshwater marsh surrounded by hardwood forest and overgrown fields. One of the largest marshes in Erie County, it's a good place to see waterfowl, deer, and tur-

tles. Fishing is allowed (with a permit).

Take Route 5 past Harris Hill to Shisler Road and turn right. Bear right at Bergtold Road and follow Shisler past Wehrle Drive, which branches off to the right, to Tillman Road on the left.

Akron Falls Park is a pleasant 284-acre county park—especially before and after the summer crowd season. A trail climbs through the woods along Murder Creek (upstream from the bridge) to a lookout on Akron Falls, where the creek crosses the Onondaga Escarpment. The park has several levels of open picnic area with tables, pavilions, and a refreshment stand. Washrooms and fresh water are also available. Swings, slides, and turnabouts are scattered throughout. There are also wooded sections along the creek where fishing (with a permit) is allowed. No fee.

Take Route 5 out to Akron Falls, at Route 93, and turn left (north). Continue on 93 for less than a mile to the Akron Falls Park sign and Parkview Drive on the right.

Como Lake Park is a 534-acre county park in the Town of Lancaster, about 11 miles east of downtown Buffalo. It lies along the banks of Cayuga Creek and includes a dam and artificial lake at its western end, which serves as a flood control reservoir in spring. This end of the park is wooded and peaceful—especially inviting on a hot summer's day.

Originally purchased by Erie County in 1925 for water-oriented, passive recreation, the park has been developed gradually. It now has 62 picnic shelters, several baseball diamonds, tennis courts, basketball courts, play equipment, restrooms, concession stands, and a newly developed nature trail. There is a casino with a fireplace, an ice skating pond, and cross-country ski trails.

See directions to Reinstein Preserve, p. 34. Take Como Park Boulevard east about four more miles to the park entrance.

Alden Town Park and Joe Panza Nature Trail: Over half of this 60-acre park, on Ellicott Creek in the Village of Alden, is a forest dominated by hemlock, beech, yellow birch, and sugar maple trees, and is home to deer, raccoon, fox, opossum, and a variety of birds and fish. Within the park, the 1½-mile Joe Panza Nature Trail, dedicated to an original member of the Alden Environmental Conservation Commission, is open year-round to nature study, hiking, picnicking, and cross-country skiing. The trail provides access to Ellicott Creek in an undisturbed setting that is becoming rare on that stream. An excellent guide book to the nature trail was developed by the Conservation Commission and may be obtained by writing to the Town of Alden, 11901 Broadway, Alden, N.Y. 14004.

A half mile upstream from the town park, in the Village of Alden, is a locally famous fossil collecting site on **Spring Creek**, which is tributary to Ellicott. Here specimens of brachiopods, corals, and trilobites are finely preserved in the Middle Devonian shale, many of them encased in iron pyrite, or "Fools' gold."

A field trip for environmental science classes could start in the morning with forest and stream ecology in the park and wind up 400 million years later with the geology exposed at Spring Creek. Kids could hunt for treasures, too!

From Buffalo, take Route 33 east to Transit Road (Route 78), and Transit Road south to Broadway (Route 20). Turn left (east) on Broadway and continue about 10 miles to the Village of Alden. In the village you will need to make a sharp left turn onto West Main Street to find the town park and nature trail entrance on your right.

The Village of East Aurora is rich in fine architecture but perhaps most famous for Elbert Hubbard's Roycroft Campus on Grove Street off Main. The Roycrofters were a part of the American arts-and-crafts movement who, like their English counterparts led by William Morris, sought to revive and develop handicrafts in an increasingly dehumanized industrial age. Today this interesting complex of buildings includes a restaurant, a weavers' supply shop, antique and gift shops, and pottery studios.

Take the Thruway (Route 90) west to Route 400 (the East Aurora Expressway) and get off at the East Aurora exit, which lands you on Route 20A. Turn right. 20A is East Aurora's Main Street. Turn left on Grove Street (near the center of town).

Emery Park (489 acres), just south of East Aurora, is a beautifully landscaped county park that accommodates a range of outdoor activities. There are trails through pine and hardwood forests along the high banks of a Cazenovia Creek tributary and a stone stairway down to the creekbed. Recreation facilities include a ski area with a lift, cross-country trails, tennis courts, and picnic areas with shelters, tables, and grills. Imaginatively equipped playgrounds are well distributed and make this a comfortable park for families with small children.

Take Route 90 west to Route 400, and 400 all the way to its end (past the East Aurora exit). Just after 400 turns into Route 16 (in South Wales), you will see Emery Road on your right. Turn right and proceed a half mile or so. There are several park entrances on either side of the road. No fee.

Hunter's Creek Wilderness: This 759-acre undeveloped county park is, perhaps intentionally, a well-kept secret. The trails and the park itself are without signs and almost impossible to find if you don't know what to look for. Hunter's Creek bisects the park and cuts a lovely gorge through part of it, but, since the creek is usually impassable, trails on both sides are accessed by two separate park entrances: one off Center Line Road, the other off Hunter's Creek Road. Altogether there are about 10 miles of hiking or cross-country ski trails that lead over high forested hills and, eventually, down to the creek.

Take Route 90 west to Route 400 and the East Aurora exit. Turn left on Route 20A and continue to Route 78 (Strykersville Road), which will branch off to the right. After a mile or so, Hunter's Creek Road intersects on the right. Turn right and cross the small bridge. The park entrance is the second right driveway after the bridge. You

will see a pond, two outhouses, and some trail markers to confirm you are there. Or you can continue up Hunter's Creek Road to Center Line Road and turn right. Trails lead in from Center Line opposite Vermont Hill Road. Park on the road.

Sprague Brook: Although this park may not look like much when you first drive in, a walk along any one of several trails reveals the pretty wooded ravines and fast-running brooks that make it a favorite with hikers and cross-country skiers. Sprague Brook is also Erie County's major camping park. Its 974 acres include 123 campsites (no electricity), with a $4.00 camping fee per family per night. There are washrooms, picnic areas, ponds for fishing, tennis courts, baseball diamonds, and easy hiking trails. These trails are only accessible by snowshoes or cross-country skis in winter; several are reserved for snowmobiles.

Take Route 240 through Glenwood to Foote Road (about one mile past Kissing Bridge) and turn left. You will see the park entrance on the left side of Foote Road.

Erie County Forest: The county began its reforestation program on these farm lots

in 1927, after severe winters had driven the last of the farmers away. There are two 1¾-mile trails through the second-growth forest. Both sections of the Conservation Trail (see p. 79) are marked by yellow paint blazes. The easy one begins south of Genesee Road just past the registration booth and has nature study stations along the way. The other, beginning across the road, leads over relatively rough terrain and has no stations. By January 1, the snow is usually deep enough for good snowshoeing or cross-country skiing. There is also a Braille Trail and a sugarhouse, where they make maple syrup in the spring. Wild berries of all kinds grow here along with jack-in-the-pulpit, trillium, columbine, and poison ivy.

White-tailed deer, rabbits, raccoon, fox, skunks, opossum, and mink may be seen in the area.

Take Route 240 south to East Concord and turn left (east) on Genesee Road. Continue about 3½ miles and park on the right side of the road. The Forestry Administration Office is a little farther down Genesee Road at Warner Gulf Road.

SOUTHERN GENESEE COUNTY

Darien Lakes State Park: This 1,845-acre park is bisected by Eleven Mile Creek, a tributary of Ellicott Creek. It is mainly undeveloped and forested, including large wetland areas. There are also picnic areas, a bathing beach, a camping area with 150 campsites (no electricity), and hiking/cross-country skiing trails. Campsites are available from early May to early September for $10.00 a day. In summer the park administration offers workshops on arts, crafts, and nature appreciation. For camp reservations and information call: 1–800–456–CAMP.

From Buffalo, take Route 20 about 21 miles east to Harlow Road and turn left. The park entrance is on your right. Or take Route 90 east to exit 48A and Route 77 south for 6½ miles.

WYOMING COUNTY

Bryncliff, about 13 miles east of the Village of East Aurora, is one of the best places for cross-country skiing in the region. Twelve and a half miles of trails, ranging from easy to "challenging," curl through a rolling terrain of field and forest. The main trails are lit at night. Overnight accommodations, food, and drinks are available at the lodge. (Call first, if you plan to dine, to be sure the restaurant is open: 716–535–7300.) You can also rent your cross-country ski equipment there. In summer, Byrncliff offers an 18-hole golf course, tennis courts, and an outdoor swimming pool. There is an admission fee.

Follow directions to East Aurora, except turn left on 20A, and continue east for 13 miles. You will see the sign for Byrncliff on your right. A nice winter's day trip could include having a late fireside lunch at the Roycroft restaurant in East Aurora (call first to be sure they're open) and then skiing into the dark at Byrncliff. For other ski touring areas, see p. 75.

Gouinlock Pond Preserve: This scenic 183-acre tract of land in Wyoming County was a gift to the Nature Conservancy from the Gouinlock family. Half of the preserve is forested with red oak, mountain ash, basswood, maple, and tulip trees mixed with pine, spruce, hemlock, and larch. The rest is fields. The mix of trees and open land provides habitat and food for a good variety of mammals and birds.

Thirty-acre Gouinlock Pond came into being in the 1930s, when beaver, then reintroduced to the area, built a dam impounding part of the marshy lowland. In the 1950s, Mr. Gouinlock built an earthen dam to stabilize the water level of the beaver pond, which now serves as a resting area for many species of migratory waterfowl. Along the preserve's eastern boundary, the dense marsh remnant receives runoff from the pond and provides homes to muskrat, mink, raccoon, and other mammals.

Take Route 20 east to Route 238. Continue on 238 southeast from Attica to Jillson Road. Turn east (left) on Jillson Road and follow it to Werner Road (right turn), which takes you through the center of the Preserve. There is one developed trail around Gouinlock Pond (trailhead on Werner Road) and interesting walks along an abandoned road or through the woods that can be taken with little difficulty.

Beaver Meadow Audubon Center:

The most immediately impressive thing about this 324-acre wildlife preserve is not the beaver (who, during the day, stay out of sight in their lodge on the pond), but the quarter-mile-long trail for the blind and the handicapped. The "Jenny Glen" trail, as it's called, is named after the daughter of David Bigelow, the Western New York naturalist who conceived it, donated part of the land, and served as Beaver Meadow's first director. A perfectly level boardwalk (with railings), it takes you through a swamp where a variety of frogs, toads, turtles, snakes, and salamanders happily live. At night the swamp is a cacophony of trills, snores, peeps, and "jug-

o-rums" punctuated by the green frog's pluck of the banjo string.

A little farther down Welch Road, the beaver pond has several short trails to and around it and a very nice visitors' center nearby. From the center's windows on one stormy April afternoon, we saw at least a dozen species of birds. Geese and other migrating waterfowl stop at the pond. Trails lead across the road to two kettle ponds, which are characteristic of the area.

The Buffalo Audubon Society maintains Beaver Meadow and conducts nature walks as well as training courses at the center in field ornithology and basic ecology. An observatory with a 12½-inch reflecting telescope is open for stargazing every Saturday night. In winter there are snowshoes for rent. In spring they make maple syrup in the sugarhouse. In summer the

"butterfly gardens" of milkweed and goldenrod are in full swing. The visitors' center is open from 10 to 5, Tuesday through Saturday, and 1 to 5 on Sunday all year round. It is closed Monday. No fee.

Take Route 90 west to Route 400 and 400 to the East Aurora exit. Turn left on 20A and continue to Route 78. Take 78 south through Strykersville to Welch Road and turn left. Continue on Welch Road across Route 77, and you will see the boardwalk trail on your left. The visitors' center and beaver pond are a bit further down on the right.

LETCHWORTH STATE PARK

Letchworth State Park (14,350 acres) is 50 miles east from Buffalo and well worth the trip. It centers on a gorge deeper than Niagara's, through which the Genesee River falls in three separate cataracts, with a combined drop of 266 feet. The original park was given to New York State by William Pryor Letchworth, a Buffalo businessman who began buying and salvaging the first 1,000 acres of river tract in 1859. (Lumber-

ing and mill operations had already taken their toll along the Genesee.) He converted the old tavern at the middle falls into an elegant house (now the Glen Iris Inn), where he lived for much of his life directing the park's landscaping and plantation.

"Gen-nis-hee-yo" in Senecan means "between beautiful fields or banks." The Genesee River Valley was long the home of the Senecas, whose garden villages were renowned for their richness and beauty.

Flora and fauna: A great variety of tree species grow here (thanks to Letchworth), along with many kinds of wildflowers, berries, and uncommon protected plants, including several species of orchid. Woodchucks, white-tailed deer, red fox, raccoons, skunks, rabbits, opossum, and many species of birds live in the park. You often see the eagle-sized turkey vulture rolling and swaying on the air currents over the gorge.

Geology: The Genesee, New York State's longest northward flowing river, took its present course as the glacier retreated from this area. Impounded melt waters of a high-level glacial lake escaped northward, the young stream cutting readily through the glacial till and becoming superimposed on the rocks below. This superimposition is visible in the valley meanders of the park's two canyonlike gorges. The miles of relatively straight and open valley between them mark where the Genesee settled more comfortably in an older (preglacial) river channel.

Late Devonian shales and sandstones make up most of the rockbeds exposed in the gorge walls, which in some places approach 600 feet in height. The Table Rock trail at the lower falls leads over a stone bridge to the east side of the gorge and provides the best close-up views of these strata.

Recreation: The eastern side of the gorge is fairly wild; the west quite developed. Trails vary accordingly in length and ease, and several of them are closed in winter. Be sure to pick up the free map and trail guide at the park's entrance. In the well-groomed middle-falls area, the Glen Iris Inn affords elegant dining and overnight accommodation from Easter Sunday through the first weekend in November (716-493-2622 for reservations). The Pioneer and Indian Museum, across the road from the inn, houses Senecan artifacts, pioneer furniture, the Pike mastodon skull, and William Letchworth's

library. A nearby side-road leads to the Old Seneca Council House (which Letchworth moved here from Caneadea) and the statue and grave of Mary Jemison, "the white woman of the Genesee," who was adopted by the Seneca as a girl and lived among them, as Deh-ge-wa-nus, in the Genesee Valley for most of her long, eventful life.

The Highbanks Recreation Area, near the park's north end, features playgrounds, several pools, picnic areas, snack bars, and hiking trails to overlooks of the Mt. Morris Dam and the Hog Back, a ridge around which the river makes a U-turn. There are cabins as well as tent and trailer campgrounds throughout the park. Guides conduct walks and workshops during the summer. The Trailside Lodge Winter Recreation Area offers cross-country skiing, snowmobiling, skating, and tubing.

For more information, write the

Genesee State Park and Recreation Region.

To get there take Route 20A east to Route 39 south for the northern Perry entrance, or farther east to Route 36 south for the Mt. Morris entrance. From 20A turn south on Route 19 in Warsaw and then onto Route 19A to reach the southernmost Portageville entrance. Or continue on Route 39 south through Castile to reach the Castile (Glen Iris Road) entrance, which is the only one open in winter. Park admission fee (but from Labor Day to Memorial Day admission is free).

The Village of Warsaw, about 10 miles west of Letchworth at the junction of routes 20A and 19, is a picturesque village noted for its fine Victorian architecture. Warsaw is the Wyoming County seat. The Honey Hill ski area is just south of here on Route 19. ∎

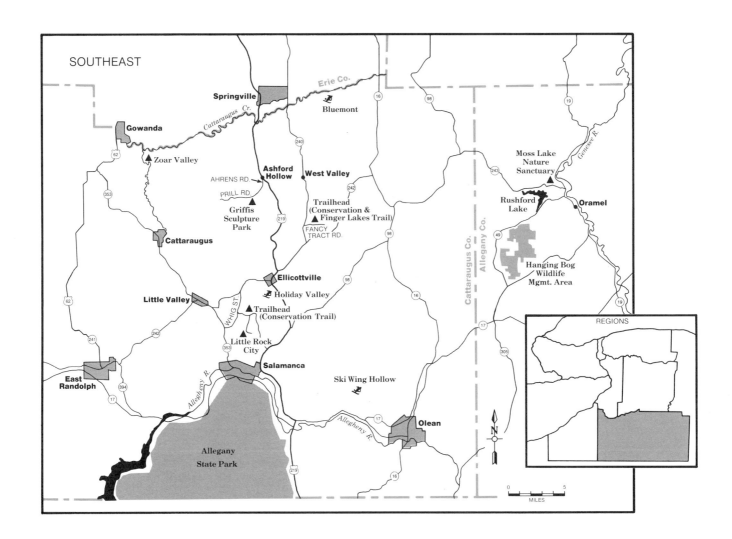

SOUTHEAST

Erie Co.

Springville

Bluemont

16

98

Gowanda

62

Zoar Valley

240

Cattaraugus Cr.

353

Ashford
Hollow

West Valley

AHRENS RD.

242

PRILL RD.

Griffis
Sculpture
Park

219

Trailhead
(Conservation &
Finger Lakes Trail)

FANCY
TRACT RD.

Cattaraugus

98

Ellicottville

Little Valley

62

WHIG ST.

Holiday Valley

98

16

242

Trailhead
(Conservation Trail)

241

Little Rock
City

353

East
Randolph

394

Salamanca

Ski Wing Hollow

17

Allegheny R.

17

Allegheny R.

17

219

Allegany
State Park

16

Moss Lake
Nature
Sanctuary

19

243

Genesee R.

Rushford
Lake

Oramel

49

Hanging Bog
Wildlife
Mgmt. Area

19

Cattaraugus Co.

Allegany Co.

305

Olean

N

0   5
MILES

REGIONS

SECTION

SOUTHEAST

The rolling hills of southern Erie and neighboring Cattaraugus counties were, some 60 million years ago, a high plateau. Centuries of erosion have carved the land into hills and valleys. Any good view of the horizon to the south (across Cattaraugus County) reveals an almost straight line—the summits marking the level of the old uplifted plain.

Ski Areas: The many downhill and cross-country ski areas that have been developed to take advantage of this terrain are popular enough not to require elaboration here. We list some of them briefly.

County- or state-maintained cross-country ski trails always open and free to the public are in Sprague Brook County Park, Erie County Forest, and Allegany State Park.*

Private ski touring centers include Byrncliff (see p. 69), Colden-Langlauf Trails (Town of Holland), Tamarack (Colden), and Holiday Valley (Ellicottville).

Private downhill ski resorts include Kissing Bridge (Glenwood), Bluemont (Yorkshire), Tamarack (Colden), Holiday Valley (Ellicottville), and Ski Wing Hollow (Allegany).

CATTARAUGUS COUNTY

Zoar Valley: This state-owned 3,500-acre strip of land along Cat-

*As you may have noticed, Allegany/Allegheny has two spellings. "Allegheny" is used for natural features: the mountains, the river, the forest, and the valley. "Allegany," sometimes called the New York spelling, applies to everything else.

taraugus Creek, southeast of Gowanda, is one of the most beautiful spots in Western New York. The Cattaraugus and its south branch have cut long narrow gorges through the Allegheny Plateau to depths of 200 feet, exposing a grand cross-section of Late Devonian shales and siltstones. ("Gowanda" comes from the Senecan "Dju-go-wan-die" meaning "below river-

cut banks.") Distinctive pie-shaped concretions up to three feet in diameter are prominent in the gorge wall and along the creek bed. The creek is stocked with trout for fishing. Its several sections of rapids attract white-water canoeists and kayakers. Wildlife is abundant.

Many Indian names and stories about the area survive. For example, it is said that a wizard, "Oat-gont," imprisoned his victims in the cave at the fork of Cattaraugus Creek and the south branch. He was finally beaten by a young man clad only in a breech cloth and moccasins. From this came the saying of "the wise ones": "Naked truth is a deep disguise which those accustomed to deceit cannot often penetrate."

Take Route 90 west to exit 57 (Hamburg), then head south on Route 62 to Gowanda. From Main Street (62) in Gowanda, turn east (left) onto Water Street after crossing the bridge over Cattaraugus Creek. Continue a half mile to Broadway (just beyond the railroad crossing) and turn right. Continue south on Broadway to Point Peter Road and turn left. There are three areas accessible from Point Peter Road:

To get to Valentine Flats, where the south branch and the main creek join, continue for about a mile on Point Peter, past the water reservoir on your right (at the bend) to the first dirt road on the left. Drive to its end, where there is a parking area. From a knife-edge trail here you may be able to see a section of the drift-filled ancestral Allegheny River Valley on the east gorge wall. An old farm road leads to a path down to the creek flats. Be careful. These paths are precipitous.

Forty Bridge crosses the south branch at a point where the creekbed is wide enough, during periods of low flow, for dry walking. You can hike upstream a mile or so to a waterfall, or downstream to where the branch and the main creek join. To get to the bridge, stay on Point Peter Road past Flats Road, but when Point Peter forks to the right, continue straight ahead down a steep winding grade to a parking area at the bridge. The Forty Bridge area is popular and a good place from which to see the steep-walled gorge.

To reach **Deer Lick Nature Sanctuary**, a 400-acre tract of land owned by the Nature Conservancy, continue on Point Peter Road when it forks right, and you will see a sign and parking area to your left. There are about 6½ miles of hiking trails here taking you through a climax forest, past a pretty falls on Deer Lick Creek, and to points overlooking Cattaraugus. Blue-winged warblers and Louisiana waterthrush nest in the area.

Another access to Cattaraugus Creek is off Route 219. Take Zoar Valley Road west to Burt's Landing. There is also a trail along the north rim of the gorge that you can reach by heading east from

Gowanda on Vail Road. The trailhead is on the right, just before the intersection with Unger Road.

Griffis Sculpture Park (Ashford Hollow):
These 400 acres of meadow and woods serve as a gallery for the metal sculptures of Buffalo artist Larry Griffis. The park is open to the public year round for picnicking, hiking, or cross-country skiing. No fee. Peter Ruszczyk, of the Foothills Trail Club, described one walk:

The first group of sculptures in sight looks like a procession: an ecclesiastic, kings, a regal-looking woman with dangling earrings. Down out of the wind, a frozen pond was surrounded by Canada geese. Then the so-called fecund female figures and, in a copse, giant animals. Proceeding on we saw the Dancing Lady, the Round Man, the Flat Man, the Deserted Man, the Observer, the Poet and the Oracle. None of these sculptures compared with the view we were getting of surrounding hills until we reached the metal maze, which the kids liked best of all. But the trails were the real maze here. We went by compass north, over icy ravines, until we

reached the hill on Prill Road which took us back to our car. (April 10, 1982)

The park has two sections: the larger one accessed by Ahrens Road off Route 219 in Ashford Hollow; the other by way of Snake Run and East Otto roads (also off 219). From the latter a trail leads uphill past a pond and picnic area (snack machines, restrooms) to a hilltop sculpture garden.

The Conservation and Finger Lakes Trails: These two foot-trails run north together from Allegany State Park to Ashford Hollow Village. There the Finger Lakes Trail heads eastward to the Catskill Mountains, and the Conservation Trail continues about 70 miles northward to Darien Lakes State Park. There are more than 400 miles of trail now completed in this system, which will eventually extend, via the Bruce Trail, to Georgian Bay in Ontario. They wind through private land, state reforestation areas, and state and county parks. Trails are marked by the standard two-by-six-inch paint blazes on trees, with double blazes indicating turns. If you plan to hike any great distance, carry water and a compass. Several state reforestation areas and county parks permit overnight camping. Outside of these areas, no camping or fires are permitted.

To reach the conjunction of the Conservation and Finger Lakes Trails, take Route 240 (West Valley Road) south about four miles past West Valley to Fancy Tract Road. Turn east (left) and, after about half a mile, start looking for white blazes (marking the Finger Lakes Trail) on the trees to your left. Park on the road. If you follow the Finger Lakes Trail about half a mile, you will see a sign for the Conservation Trail (orange blazes) north, while the Finger Lakes Trail continues east.

For more information and for detailed maps of these trails, write to: Finger Lakes Trail Conference Service Center, P.O. Box 18048, Rochester, N.Y. 14618; or, for the Conservation Trail, contact Foothills Trail Club, c/o Mary Dillon, 60 May Road, Elma, N.Y. 14059.

Little Rock City, in Little Valley, is one of several similar rock formations across the southern part of Western New York. Alternate periods of freezing and thawing over two million years of glaciation widened the stress fractures in these rocks, splitting them apart. The resulting gigantic blocks have long since been weathered and covered with

lichens and moss. You can walk under rock bridges, squeeze through rock crannies, or leap across the roofs.

Take Route 219 south to Ellicottville, and Route 242 west from Ellicottville for three miles to Whig Street, which branches off on the left. Two miles up this road turn left at the Whig Street Church onto Hungry Hollow Road (unmarked). Continue about one mile, and you'll see a dirt road with trail markers crossing your road. This is a section of the Conservation Trail. Park on the road and hike in on the right-hand trail about two miles to Little Rock City. There is also a trail in from the Elkdale Country Club (take Route 353 south from Ellicottville to Elkdale).

Caution: This is a popular deer-hunting area in fall.

There is another "rock city" south of

Olean (off Route 16) as well as Thunder Rocks in Allegany State Park and Panama Rocks in Chautauqua County. The Olean and Panama rock parks are privately owned and charge admission.

Salamanca is the only city in the United States built on an Indian reservation. In 1892 white settlers signed a 99-year lease with the Senecas to protect their property. (A new lease is being negotiated as this book goes to press.)

The **Seneca Nation Museum** is on Broad Street at the west end of Salamanca. The museum's purpose, according to Curator George Abrahams, is "to identify, collect, preserve, display and interpret to the general public ideas, objects, artifacts and natural cultural treasures related to Iroquois people." The museum has a shop with books on Indian history and culture as well as contemporary Iroquois artwork for sale.

ALLEGANY STATE PARK

Allegany State Park is the largest in the state park system. Covering over 65,000 acres, it is flanked on the west and north-

east by the Allegany Indian Reservation, and on the south, in Pennsylvania, by the 470,000-acre Allegheny National Forest. The Holland Land Company gained title to the New York lands (except the Allegany Indian Reservation) with the Treaty of Big Tree in 1787. Quakers established the first white settlement in 1803, in what

are now park grounds, when they opened a school for Indians at Tunesassah. Other 19th-century settlements were mainly lumber camps, which came and went with timber supplies. In 1921 the State of New York designated 7,000 acres of this threatened timberland a state park. Since then Allegany has steadily grown with the state's acquisition of neighboring lands from private owners.

Geology: The park occupies most of that region in southern Cattaraugus County within the loop of the Allegheny River, which enters New York State at the southeastern corner of the county, swings north for several miles, and then crosses back into Pennsylvania near the southwest corner of the county. This roughly triangular highland—the geographers call it "the Salamanca Re-entrant"—is the only section of Western New York that, for the most part, escaped glaciation. Local relief, therefore, is comparatively high, elevations differing by as much as 500 feet within a square mile. Valleys are generally V-shaped, being free of glacial fill and glacial scouring. The slopes are long and steep.

The oldest layer of exposed bedrock in the park is the Chadakoin Formation of the Late Devonian Period. You will find an easily accessible outcrop at Elko Mountain by the mouth of Wolf Run, where a roadcut has exposed the purplish shales of this formation. The youngest formation is the Olean Conglomerate, made up of quartz and spar pebbles deposited here in the early Pennsylvania Period and then compressed, over millions of years, into rock. The Olean Conglomerate can be seen at Thunder Rocks, an assemblage of monoliths that was formed in the same way as those in Little Valley, Olean, and Panama (see "Little Rock City," p. 79).

Fauna: Forest mammals inhabiting the park include white-tailed deer, black bear, raccoons, porcupines, woodchucks, cottontail rabbits, fox, and several species of squirrel, mole, and other small rodents. Barred and great-horned owls, red-tailed, broad-winged, and sharp-shined hawks are among the predatory birds to be seen. Ruffed grouse and wild turkey are plentiful, as are a variety of marsh birds, including many kinds of ducks, great blue and green heron, and red-winged blackbirds. An industrious population of beavers is largely responsible for the wetlands within the park.

Recreation facilities concentrate around two large lakes: Red House in the north, and Quaker in the southern part of the park. These areas have lodges, restaurants, athletic fields, tennis courts, and swimming pools. Concessioners rent boats, canoes, bicycles, and ski equipment. A general store and laundry in each section make "roughing it" next to impossible for campers in the park.

Each area has cabins and trailer and tent camps, but only Red House is open all year round. (Quaker is open from April 1 to December 15.) Altogether there are about 400 individual cabins ranging in size and amenities, but all basically equipped with a gas stove, a refrigerator, and a wood-burning stove for heat. For campsite and cabin reservations, write New York State Parks and Recreation, Allegany Region, Red House Rental Office, RD 1, Salamanca, N.Y. 14779, or call 716-354-4585.

Trails: Because of the concentration of recreational facilities, most visitors never see the remaining 90 percent of the park—the part most worth seeing. Be sure then, when you enter Allegany, to pick up a guide map on which the 16 trails penetrating less populated sec-

tions are clearly numbered and marked. The longest, "North Country Trail," joins the trail of the same name, which runs through Allegheny National Forest to the Conservation-Finger Lakes Trail in the north (see p. 79). "Ridgerun Trail" is the most remote, taking you through pine forests and past "the summit," the highest point in the park. Or you can take one of the old logging roads for a tranquil and solitary walk. Park naturalists conduct nature-interpretation walks along many of these trails during the summer. In the winter there are ski touring trails near Red House Lake.

Since its beginning, Allegany has been developed as a "resource and recreation park," which means that it is still open to resource exploitation. Hunting, trapping, lumbering, and oil and gas drilling all take place within the park. Hiking trails through areas posted for hunting are best avoided in hunting season.

There is a park admission fee from Memorial Day to Labor Day. To get there, take Route 219 south to Route 17 (the Southern Tier Expressway) and head west. Exits 18 and 19 bring you to park entrances.

ALLEGANY COUNTY

Moss Lake Nature Sanctuary is about 65 miles southeast of Buffalo, in the northwest corner of Allegany County. Its preservation led to the establishment of the Nature Conservancy's Western New York chapter in 1958. The 81-acre parcel of land contains a bog lake in a kettle hole, once filled with a block of ice left by the retreating glacier. Various bog plants and mosses became established along the edge of the kettle hole, forming, eventually, the sphagnum moss mat that has filled in and covered much of the open water.

Specialized plants like the sundew, cran

Wild flowers:
(1) Trillium.
(2) Wild ginger.
(3) True Soloman's seal.
(4) False Soloman's seal.
(5) Pitcher plant.

berry, leatherleaf, and pitcher plant grow in this acidic bog environment. Other plant communities surround the bog: an oak woods, a beech-birch-maple-hemlock forest, and fields in different stages of succession. Over 75 species of birds have been recorded at the sanctuary, which was designated as a National Natural Landmark in 1973. The Biology Department of nearby Houghton College uses Moss Lake as an outdoor laboratory.

There are trails around the lake and around several dry kettles in the woodlands. If you go in maple-sugaring season, stop along the way at Moore's Pancake House, on Galen Hill Road, nine miles south of Arcade, for all-you-can-eat homemade pancakes and pure maple syrup from their own sugarbush.

To get to Moss

Lake from Buffalo, take the Thruway (Route 90) to Route 400, and 400 to Route 20A. Head east on 20A for about 29 miles to Warsaw, and then south about 25 miles on Route 19 to Houghton. From the intersection of 19 and Genesee Street in Houghton, continue 1½ miles south on Route 19 to Sand Hill Road and turn right. Drive a mile up the hill. Moss Lake is on the left-hand side. You are in the Genesee River Watershed; Route 19 follows along the west bank of the Genesee.

Hanging Bog Wildlife Management Area:

Hanging Bog Wildlife Management Area: Located in the Town of New Hudson, Allegany County, Hanging Bog Wildlife Management Area is one of the largest (4,571 acres) wildlife areas managed by the Department of Environmental Conservation in Western New York. As with most other state-owned undeveloped property, the land originally reverted from private to public ownership in the 1930s, after the Resettlement Act enabled the federal government to buy out bankrupt farmers. (This explains why we own so many hilltops, swamps, and other poor sites for farms.) It was transferred to the state in 1962.

The distinctive feature of the area is a 20-acre bog, which is mostly open water with some characteristic bog plants such as sundew, leatherleaf, and a few rarer species. Rush Creek and Crawford Creek, tributaries to the Genesee River, run through the property. Management practices have included planting of conifers, selective and clear cutting of hardwoods, leasing of croplands, planting of wildlife shrubs, and developing ponds, potholes, and small marshes to provide food and habitat to a select variety of wildlife. Hunting is a major factor in this selection. White-tailed deer, cottontail rabbit, gray squirrel, ruffed grouse, woodcock, raccoon, red and gray fox, opossum, and several species of waterfowl are common to the area.

There are nine designated camping aeas with no facilities. If you wish to camp, you can reserve a space by calling the Department of Environmental Conservation's Olean office at 716–372–8678. They will send you a map. There is no fee for camping.

Unless you are a hunter, stay away from the area during hunting seasons. At other times of the year, you may hike around on old truck trails. There are no nature trails per se.

To get there, follow directions to Moss Lake, but continue on Route 19 to Oramel, where you pick up Route 49. Turn west (right) on 49, which takes you along the south side of Rushford Lake and to Rush Creek Road. On Rush Creek Road you will pass Slusher Hill Road (dirt) on your left. About two miles past Slusher Hill, you reach New Hudson Road, which runs through the center of state land. Turn left. Hanging Bog is about 1½ miles down this road, on the left. You can park along this road or any of the several town roads or truck trails leading off it. ■

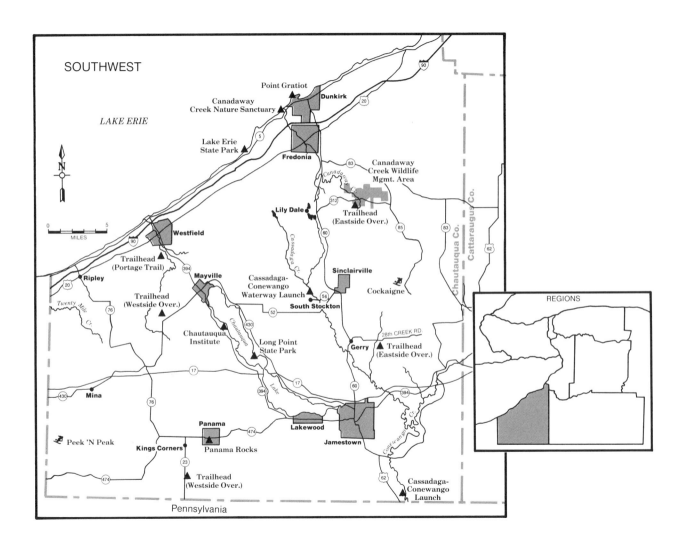

SOUTHWEST

LAKE ERIE

Point Gratiot
Canadaway
Creek Nature Sanctuary
Dunkirk

Lake Erie
State Park
Fredonia

Canadaway
Creek Wildlife
Mgmt. Area

Lily Dale
Trailhead
(Eastside Over.)

Westfield

Trailhead
(Portage Trail)
Ripley
Mayville
Sinclairville
Cockaigne

Twenty Mile Cr.
Trailhead
(Westside Over.)
Cassadaga-
Conewango
Waterway Launch
South Stockton

Chautauqua
Institute
Long Point
State Park
28th CREEK RD.
Gerry
Trailhead
(Eastside Over.)

Mina

Peek 'N Peak
Panama
Kings Corners
Panama Rocks
Lakewood
Jamestown

Trailhead
(Westside Over.)
Cassadaga-
Conewango
Launch

Pennsylvania

Chautauqua Co.
Cattaraugus Co.

REGIONS

ERIE LAKESHORE

Dunkirk: This city is at the heart of the grape belt—the vineyards you see all along Chautauqua's Lake Erie shore. Along with the familiar Concord, there are wine grapes—Delaware, French hybrid Siebel— to supply the several wineries in the area. (Most of these give tasting tours, which the Dunkirk Chamber of Commerce can tell you about.) Dunkirk Harbor, once a busy commercial port, is now mainly used by pleasure craft, though some commercial fishing is still done from here. A picturesque lighthouse, built in 1827, sits on Point Gratiot, and Point Gratiot Park has picnic areas and bathing beaches.

Take Route 90 west to exit 59 and follow Route 60 north to Route 5. A left on Route 5 brings you to the harbor.

Canadaway Creek Nature Sanctuary, owned by the Nature Conservancy, borders Canadaway Creek at its confluence with Lake Erie. Typifying the Conservancy's policy for preserving "the last of the least and the best of the rest," the sanctuary represents one of the few undeveloped green spaces left along Lake Erie between Presque Isle, in Pennsylvania, and Buffalo's Tifft Farm. As such, the 32.6-acre area is an important stopover for migrating birds. Over 160 species of birds have been identified here, including black-crowned night heron, whistling swan, brant, wood duck, willet, red

phalarope, caspian tern, tufted titmouse, carolina wren, and 22 species of warblers. A good time to visit is during spring or fall migration.

The Indian name for "Canadaway" was "Ganadawao," which means "stream among the hemlocks." Apparently the area was the site of an Erie and, later, an Iroquois village. The land has a history of farming and flooding, and is now dominated by black willows, alder, and wild grape.

Take Route 90 southwest from Buffalo to exit 59 (Dunkirk). Turn right on Bennett Road (Route 60) and drive into Dunkirk to Lake Shore Drive (Route 5). Turn left and proceed about 2½ miles to the sanctuary. Park along Route 5 or turn onto Temple Road, and you will see a parking area and a sign. There are trails from these roads.

Lake Erie State Park, about seven miles southwest of Dunkirk (on Route 5), is characteristic of this part of Chautauqua County, with pine and hardwood-forested hills sloping down to a sandy beach. It has 95 campsites, 33 with electricity, and several cabins (you provide linens, etc.). The park provides potable water, washrooms, and chopped wood (for a fee), but no stores or snackbars. Recreational facilities include a lifeguarded beach with a bathhouse, picnic areas, and playgrounds. A woodland "nature interpretation trail" begins near the swings. Admission fee.

Westfield: This village full of antique shops is about 15 miles south of Dunkirk. The county's first permanent white settler had a home on the site now occupied by the Chautauqua County Historical Society Museum, just south of the junction of routes 17 and 20. There are several other interesting places right around the village. **Barcelona Harbor,** for example, has a 500-foot-long pier, protected by a distant breakwall, which provides mooring for hundreds of small craft. It is also known for its smokehouse, where Lake Erie whitefish are cured over smouldering corn cobs. There are seafood restaurants nearby. Ottaway Park, a 107-acre village park on Tupper Creek at the lake, is exceptionally lovely—especially on weekdays, when it is not heavily used. A hiking trail down to the creek brings you through groves of pine and spiney honey locusts. You may see cone-in-cone concretions in the shales along the shore. There are picnic areas and playgrounds. From Memorial Day to the Fourth of July, this park is open only on weekends. But from July 4 to Labor Day it is open every day. Admission fee for non-Westfield residents. Ottaway Park is accessed by Route 5.

To reach Westfield, take Route 90 west to exit 60.

Portage Trail: Seneca Indians portaged their canoes over this 13-mile-long trail to get from Lake Erie to Lake Chautauqua, and from there to the Mississippi River. (Chautauqua Lake, formed when glacial drift blocked a Lake Erie-trending valley stream, is part of the Mississippi drainage by way of the Chadakoin River.) A pleasant hike along this trail begins on Gale Street, outside of Westfield, and takes you to Buttermilk Falls, in the Little Chautauqua Creek Gorge. The trail continues over moderately hilly terrain, with some sections following country roads, all the way to Mayville, the Chautauqua County seat, at the northern end of Chautauqua Lake. However, be forewarned, the trail is not always well maintained and may be hard to follow in places.

Take Route 90 west to Westfield (exit 60) and turn south on Route 394. Go through Westfield. Take the first right turn outside the village limits onto Gale Street. You will see a trail entrance marker on the right. This trail may also be picked up at many points in Mayville.

CHAUTAUQUA COUNTY, NORTH

Canadaway Creek Wildlife Management Area, six miles southeast of Fredonia, encompasses 2,180 acres of steep wooded hills and several small creeks, the main one being Canadaway. The New York State Department of Environmental Conservation maintains trails and dirt roads through the area, including a section of the Eastside Overland Trail. Route 312 is the main access road, running more or less through the center, with parking areas and trailheads clearly marked along its sides. Trails take you along the creek and through beautiful hardwood forests with pine plantations and the occasional orchard-gone-wild. From the top of at least one summit, you can see Lake Erie shimmering in the distance. Ball Road (unmarked), the first road on the left after passing the area headquarters on the right, follows Canadaway Creek for a few miles. The road is closed to vehicles, but there is a trail with several spurs. Across Route 312 and for the next few miles you will see other trails into the woods. Another section can be reached from Center Road (continue on 312 to the old cheese factory and turn left onto Center Road). Center brings you to the north part of Ball Road (turn left), which turns into Park Road (left again). There are several trails from Park Road.

Caution: This would be a hazardous place to walk in hunting season. White-tailed deer, cottontail rabbits, varying hare, squirrel, fox squirrel, red and gray fox, woodcock, wild turkeys, ruffed grouse, and several species of ducks inhabit the area.

To get there, take Route 90 west to Fredonia (exit 59) and Route 60 about eight miles south to Route 312, the first road to the left after Shumla Road. Turn left (east) and follow this road for about three miles to the Canadaway Creek Wildlife Management Area signs.

Eastside Overland Trail:
This 19-mile-long trail, developed by the Chautauqua County Parks Commission, runs from the Canadaway Creek Wildlife Management Area almost to the City of Jamestown. The trail is mainly through state or county forest, but in some places runs alongside roads or privately owned lands. There are two lean-to camping sites, both on county land in the Canadaway Creek area.

The north end trailhead is off Route 312 (72), 1½ miles east of Hall Road. From here, the trail heads southeast to 28th Creek Road, about three miles east of the Village of Gerry. For a map, write to the Chautauqua County Parks Commission, Gerace Office Building, Mayville, N.Y. 14757.

Lily Dale: The spiritualist center at Lily Dale, on the Cassadaga Lakes, is surely the only place of its kind in the world, which is why we have included it in this guide. Every summer, from late June through the end of August, the Lily Dale Assembly holds a spiritualist conference in this tiny community that attracts mediums from all over the country. The public is invited to join them—for lectures and demonstrations on mediumship, healing services, and consultations. Lily Dale boasts 45 registered mediums, who advertise their skills on shingles hanging from their porches. Anyone interested can arrange for a reading or a group seance any time of the year. Lily Dale also has a research library, two hotels, a cafeteria, picnic pavilions, a camping area (no tents), and a pet cemetery. The village itself, a smaller, less prosperous-looking version of Chautauqua, seems to have stopped in time about a century ago.

Take Route 90 west to Fredonia (exit 59) and Route 60 south about 8½ miles to Dale Road (you will see the sign saying "Lily Dale 1 Mile"). Turn right. During the summer there is an admission fee at the entrance gate to this community.

CHAUTAUQUA: THE INSTITUTE & THE LAKE

The Chautauqua Institute was founded in 1874 as a center for learning and the arts. In addition to the campus established on Lake Chautauqua, the Institute sent out bands of scholars and artists into the American countryside to educate and entertain the populace. A chautauqua in Ohio or Wisconsin or Arkansas was a summer cultural program, a series of lectures and concerts, and for many poor farmers and struggling townfolk this chautauqua would be the bright spot of the long, hard year. Now Chautauqua has the settled look of a prosperous 19th-century American town. Narrow streets, handsome wooden houses, spreading trees, an idyllic town square

with a shady green and plenty of benches—the sense of all this on a summer's day is peaceful and deeply satisfying. And yet Chautauqua is still very much of a thriving concern, a cultural and artistic center bustling with events and activities.

Each summer season the Chautauqua Institute invites internationally known artists to join with the resident symphony orchestra, opera company, and theater company for an outstanding series of concerts and performances. A continuing lecture program features distinguished authors, scientists, politicians, and philosophers discussing the major questions of our society today. Visiting performing artists and craftsmen give master classes and workshops. And the Chautauqua summer school offers a variety of formal courses, ranging from foreign languages to creative writing.

The grounds include a 5,000-seat amphitheater, an opera house, classrooms, residence halls, a library, and several outdoor auditoriums. There is also a pleasant swimming beach, tennis courts, and an 18-hole golf course. Restaurants, cafeterias, and shops are open in season, as well as several hotels and guest houses. There are also furnished apartments available for rent. Write Chautauqua Institution, Box 1095, Chautauqua, N.Y. 14722, or call 716–357–5635 for an accommodations brochure or a summer program.

In the off-season, this village with its old, quiet charm is still well worth a visit—and you won't have to pay admission at the gate. To get there, take Route 90 west to exit 60 (Westfield) and Route 17 southeast to Mayville. In Mayville pick up Route 394, which brings you, after about three miles, to the gates of Chautauqua.

Chautauqua Lake:

This pretty 17-mile-long lake is surrounded by summer cottages, a few old estates with mansions, and the villages of Mayville, Lakewood,

Celoron, and, of course, Chautauqua. On any fine day, just about every imaginable kind of watersport goes on here. Besides the normal run of sailboats, yachts, canoes, kayaks, and outboards with waterskiers attached, there is a paddle-wheel steamer, *The Chautauqua Belle,* for excursions around the lake (board at Mayville). Anglers, in boats or along the piers, try for muskellunge, the specialty fish of this lake, as well as for bass, walleye, and crappie. Kids in huge rubber inner-tubes, on "Sunfish," or on surfboards holding sails, float in little schools around the Chautauqua Institute or breeze along the beaches. There are a few public beaches around the lake, the largest at Long Point State Park, which has a lifeguard, a bathhouse, playgrounds, picnic facilities, a grocery, and a marina, but no overnight camping. There is a fee. Long Point State Park is accessed by Route 17.

"Chautauqua" comes from the Seneca word "Cha-da-que," which has at least two meanings: "lifting-out-of-fish," referring to a story about the muskellunge; and "fog," which often deeply shrouds the lake and shore at night.

CHAUTAUQUA COUNTY, SOUTH

Panama Rocks: For families with older children, an excursion to the site of Panama Rocks makes an unusual and exciting adventure. Here your child will find a safe but spine-tingling natural labyrinth of caves and deep crevices. Some caves are indeed dark and spooky, but daylight is always near. You will find cool cavern breezes and sequestered moss-hung nooks—good places for brief meditation.

The Eries and later the Iroquois sheltered among these rocks, storing their meat in ice caves deep in the ridge. Local legend has it that there is a gold shipment buried somewhere here, hidden and then lost by the robbers of a bank in nearby Clymer. (Any gold nuggets found must be turned in at the gates upon leaving!)

The rocks themselves are a conglomerate of tiny quartz and spar pebbles, like those at Thunder Rocks and Olean's Rock City. Earth stresses caused the 60-foot-thick mass to fracture; the cracks widened into alleyways during the alternate periods of freezing and thawing throughout the glacial age. From above, the holes and crevices are almost hidden by forest floor cover. Be careful up there.

Panama Rocks is privately owned. The park grounds (67 acres) include a picnic grove, a snack bar, a gift shop, washrooms, and tent and trailer campsites (some with electricity and water hook-ups). There is an admission fee.

Nearby is the village of Panama, which has been called the "American Athens" because of the Greek-style architecture characteristic of its houses.

Take Route 90 west to Westfield (exit 60) and Route 17 south to Mayville. In Mayville pick up Route 394 and continue south toward Lakewood. About a mile before Lakewood, turn right onto Route 474, which brings you to Panama. Panama Rocks is in Panama, about one block south of Route 474 on Rock Hill Road.

Cassadaga-Conewango Waterway:

Chautauqua County has developed a 56-mile canoe route on these tributaries to the Allegheny River. The waterway traverses half the county from north to south, following a route used by Indians and early explorers to the Allegheny and the Ohio Country beyond. Both creeks are "flat water," making for easy paddling. However, be prepared to portage around fallen trees and snags, especially in spring.

There are parking areas and launch sites at many bridge crossings as well as lean-to shelters on a county-owned island in Conewango Creek and on several parcels of county land along the west bank of Cassadaga Creek. The northernmost launch site is at South Stockton where Route 71 crosses Cassadaga Creek. Take Route 60 south to Sinclairville and Route 52/56 west to South Stockton. In South Stockton, turn north on Route 342 (71) and you will see the bridge. Other put-in spots on Cassadaga Creek are at Red Bird, Gerry (on the Miller Road bridge), and Ross Mills. There is a lean-to for camping about a mile downstream from the Miller Road launch. You can enter Conewango Creek on the Route 42 bridge just east of Poland Center, at the Route 62 bridge about two miles east of Frewsburg, or at the south end of the waterway at the Pennsylvania border. Here county land provides canoe access, plus an island site with a lean-to for camping. Take Route 60 south through Jamestown to Route 62, and 62 about five more miles south past Frissell Road. The county launch site is on the east side of 62, about a mile past Frissell Road.

There is no fee and no advance registration necessary. However, be sure to sign in at the registration boxes provided at most of the launch sites. A map of the waterway is available from the Chautauqua County Parks Commission.

Westside Overland Trail:

The Chautauqua County Parks Commission developed and maintains this 26-mile hiking trail from Mayville to Panama. It passes through state reforestation areas, county lands, and private properties, crossing several creeks. The most spectacular section is at the north (Mayville) end, where the trail follows the steep-walled Chautauqua Creek Gorge, whose sheer canyons of shale reach heights of 200 feet. There are two lean-tos on different state-owned sections of the trail, one near Warner Road in the township of Harmony, the other near Titus Road in the township of Chautauqua. Overnight camping is permitted at these sites for a maximum of 24 hours.

Take Route 430 west from Mayville to Summerdale. Just beyond Summerdale you will see Summerdale Road on the right. Proceed north on Summerdale for about a mile to the trail on either side of the road. Take the left-hand (west) trail to reach Chautauqua Gorge. Another access to the gorge is farther west on Route 430 from Putnam Road. To get to the southern or Panama end of the trail, take Route 474 west from Panama to Town Line Road and turn left (south). The trail begins on the left (east) side of Town Line Road about a mile past Brownell Road, or about 4½ miles south of Route 474.

For a trail map, contact the Chautauqua County Parks Commission.

Private downhill ski resorts

in Chautauqua County include Peek 'N Peak in the town of French Creek, on Route 426 south of Findley Lake, and Cockaigne in the town of Cherry Creek, off Route 60 east of Sinclairville. ■

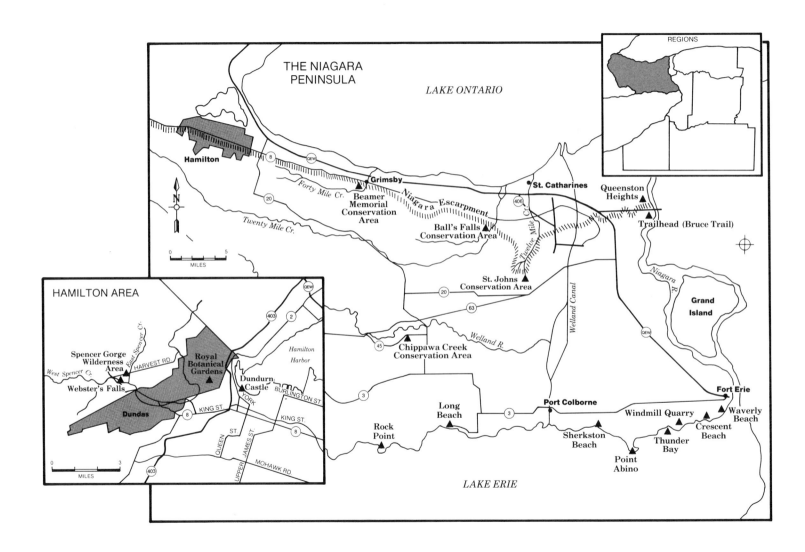

THE NIAGARA PENINSULA

FORT ERIE

The British built Fort Erie in 1764 to establish their military dominance of the Niagara Frontier and to help them control the trade between colonists and the Indians to the west. Stationed where Lake Erie flows into the Niagara River, the fort was a strategic British stronghold during the Revolutionary War and the War of 1812. It was captured by the Americans in 1814, a year after an invading British force burned Buffalo to the ground, and then returned to British control by the terms of the Treaty of Ghent. Now set in the midst of a beautifully landscaped park, Fort Erie is a pleasant bicycle ride from Buffalo (be sure to carry some identification for crossing the Peace Bridge). The soldiers' quarters, kitchen, arsenal, and jail are fully restored. There is a small museum housing blunderbusses and other historical weapons, along with many old photographs and maps of this area. "British guards" in period uniform perform military drills and fire off the cannon several times a day during the summer.

Facilities include restrooms, picnic areas, a snackbar, and a souvenir shop. There is an admission fee.

To get there, cross the Peace Bridge and take the Fort Erie exit, which brings you to Central Avenue. Take Central Avenue south to Dominion Road (Highway 3C) and follow Dominion Road a mile or two to the fort.

The present town of Fort Erie offers a modest little beach for wading, several interesting specialty shops, and a number of well-known and much-frequented Chinese restaurants. The Fort Erie racetrack is one of the oldest and prettiest horseracing courses in North America.

LAKE ERIE BEACHES

Public beaches along the north (Canadian) shore of Lake Erie become nicer and less crowded as you head west from the Peace Bridge. All are accessed by secondary roads off Highway 3, which you reach by crossing the Peace Bridge and taking the first (Fort Erie) exit. An alternative and prettier route to any beach this side (east) of Point Abino is along Dominion Road (Highway 3C), which runs parallel to Highway 3 a few blocks south. We list them in the order they come as you drive west from Buffalo. Most of them are within a 45-minute drive from central Buffalo. Allow yourself extra traveling time for heavy traffic at the Peace Bridge on holidays or when the horses are running at the Fort Erie racetrack.

Waverly Beach is the first public Lake Erie beach you come to after you pass the old fort on Dominion Road. Turn left onto Helena Street and drive to the end where you will find a parking area. Waverly offers a great view of the Buffalo skyline, and is fun to explore—particularly as you will find the remains of an old amusement park and swimming pool built right into the lake. In June the cottonwood trees that shade the picnic areas are famous for snowing the place over with their white downy fluff. Waverly Beach has a snackbar, bar, and restrooms.

Crescent Beach,

primarily for residents and cottagers, also has a small free public beach. There are no facilities here and no refreshment stand. Take Crescent Road south (left) from Highway 3 or Dominion Road.

Windmill Quarry: The water in this deep stone quarry is cold and clear, but the drop-off is sharp, so we don't recommend it for young children. There are washrooms, a refreshment stand, grassy, shaded picnic areas, and a sand beach. Admission is charged. Located off Stonemill Road, south of Highway 3.

Thunder Bay, another beach mostly for residents, does have a small free public beach with washrooms and a hotdog stand. This beach tends to be crowded and littered at the height of the season. Take Bernard Road south from Highway 3.

Point Abino: The Buffalo Canoe Club, founded in 1882, is located here. They have hosted sailboat races, including the North American Lightning Championships, for many years. Off Point Abino Road.

Sherkston Beaches and Quarry:

Famous for its three sand-duned beaches, Sherkston has long been popular with the high-school and college crowds. Parking on the beach is permitted. This is convenient, but also makes for more noise and less elbowroom.

Legend has it that the quarry—deep, clear, and *cold*—filled up overnight when earthmovers struck an underground stream years back. The belief that there is still a train down there, along with reports of other interesting wreckage, attracts scuba divers every year. The quarry is life-guarded and has a slide, a high diving board, and rafts to swim out to. There are washrooms, a bathhouse, a refreshment stand, and tent and trailer campgrounds. There is an admission fee.

Take Highway 3, about 15 miles west from the Peace Bridge, to Regional Road 98 and turn left (south). There are plenty of big signs pointing the way.

Long Beach: See "Long Beach Conservation Area," p. 104.

Rock Point Provincial Park, owned and managed by the Ontario Ministry of Natural Resources, offers camping, swimming, hiking, picnicking, and boating along a rocky stretch of Lake Erie shore (boat rental facilities are nearby). Rock Point has 89 regular campsites, 40 with electricity. The daily fee per campsite ranges between $11 and $15 with a $4 additional charge for reservations.

To make reservations, call 416-774-6642.

Take Highway 3 west from Fort Erie almost to Dunnville. Just east of Dunnville you will see signs for Rock Point, which is accessed by Niece Road.

ST. CATHARINES AREA

The Welland Canal: At the southwest end of Lake Ontario, the city of St. Catharines is probably best known as the northern terminus of the Welland Canal. The Welland Canal links the Great Lakes and North America's heartland, by way of the St. Lawrence Seaway, to the Atlantic coast. Through a series of eight locks, the canal circumvents Niagara's falls and provides a deep waterway system for lake- and ocean-going vessels to navigate from Lake Erie to Lake Ontario. The canal is 27 feet deep and accomplishes a descent of 326.5 feet—the difference in elevation between the two lakes. In 1989, 954 salties and 2,644 lakers passed through the canal.

If you want more of these amazing facts (!), visit Lock 3 with its Welland Canal Viewing Complex, historical museum, and gift shop where you may learn while watching the ships pass by. From the QEW, take the Glendale Avenue (Route 89) exit and Glendale Avenue to Government Road where you turn right (north). Follow signs to Lock 3. Government Road runs along the west side of the canal. A left (south) turn onto Government brings you to Locks 4, 5, and 6.

Festivals: St. Catharines celebrates every season with a festival. They have a Salmon Derby in April, a Folk Arts Festival in May, a Strawberry Festival in June, a Sausage Festival in July, a Grape and Wine Festival in September, and a Pumpkinfest in October. The fruit and vegetable festivities center around the **farmers' market,** a great place to find local produce all year round in downtown St. Catharines. In August, the city hosts the 100-year-old Royal Canadian Henley Regatta, featuring world-class rowing competitions on the famous Henley Course at Port Dalhousie.

Port Dalhousie, St. Catharines' picturesque harborfront village, was the terminus for the first three Welland Canals before the last one was built a mile or so to the east. The Merritt Trail, a network

of biking and walking trails following former canal routes, starts in Dalhousie.

NIAGARA PENINSULA CONSERVATION AREAS

The Niagara Peninsula Conservation Authority owns or leases 34 con-servation areas on the Niagara Peninsula as part of its water man-agement program. According to its bro-chure, "the Authority has assumed the re-sponsibility of conserv-ing, restoring, develop-ing and managing the natural resources [within the Niagara Peninsula]. Since its establishment [in 1959], this Authority has purchased over 4,500 acres of land for conservation pur-poses." These lands are used for water quality protection, for conserving unique flora and fauna, for various forest, fish, and wildlife management programs, and for recreation—including swimming, camp-ing, hiking, canoeing, picnicking, and nature studies.

For more information on Conserva-tion Authority facilities and programs call 416–227–1013.

The Bruce Trail is a 480-mile-long foot-path that follows the Niagara Escarpment from Queenston Heights, on the Niagara River, to Tobermory, on Georgian Bay. Owned by a variety of public agencies and private landowners, the trail is maintained by the Bruce Trail Association, whose headquarters are at the Royal Botanical Garden's Arboretum in Hamilton. The Bruce Trail runs through numerous large escarpment preservation areas and offers overnight camping at designated sites. A guide is available from the Trail Associa-tion. For more information call 416–529–6821 (Hamilton headquarters) or 416–468–4013 (Niagara-on-the-Lake regional office).

Ball's Falls Conservation Area, a few miles west of St. Catharines near Vineland, is a 210-acre natural and cultural preserve centering on two waterfalls and the re-mains of an early 19th-century industrial hamlet. Surviving from the once thriving complex of mills and related operations that dominated the site are the family home of George Ball, a grist mill, and a restored lime kiln. Several other historical structures have been relocated to the site. The core property remained in the hands

of the Ball family for over four generations.

After purchasing the original 1,200 acres of land in 1807, George Ball built a grist mill, saw mill, and woolen mill on the property, leading to the establishment of one of the first communities on lower Twenty Mile Creek. The grist mill is still operative, though run electrically; occasionally the giant mill wheels can be seen in motion, grinding wheat for sale. Low flows in Twenty Mile Creek, attributed to the cutting of trees and draining of swamps as the watershed was developed, led to the closing of the mills.

Twenty Mile Creek falls over the Niagara Escarpment here, creating a 90-foot cataract and another 35-foot falls a little farther upstream. The rock units exposed in the gorge represent almost the complete sequence of Silurian stratigraphy of the Niagara Peninsula.

Hiking trails through the area include the Cataract Trail and a two-mile section of the Bruce Trail along the Niagara Escarpment. Trail descriptions and information on local flora, fauna, geology, and history are displayed near the falls overlook. There are picnic areas, restrooms, and an arboretum, containing an array of unusual tree specimens.

An admission fee is charged during summer hours (from 10 to 4, mid-May to early September). The site is owned by the Niagara Peninsula Conservation Authority and is part of their watershed protection program for the land area between lakes Erie and Ontario.

Take the QEW west from St. Catharines to exit 57. This lands you on Victoria Avenue, which you follow south, through typical Niagara Peninsula orchard country for about three miles. As the road heads up the escarpment, you will see a sign for Ball's Falls, where you turn left. The parking area is just down this road on the right.

St. Johns Conservation Area: Besides Ball's Falls, the Niagara Peninsula Conservation Authority owns or leases eight other conservation areas along the Niagara Escarpment. One is St. Johns, near Fonthill, Ontario, about 15 miles west of Niagara Falls. The 76-acre site is predominated by a natural stand of hardwood forest—including many broad-leafed species typical of the Carolinian Forest Region found further south. Carolinian Forest species, in fact, are prevalent in most of the escarpment woodland on the Niagara Peninsula.

St. Johns Conservation Area forms the headwaters of Twelve Mile Creek, historically noted for its quality trout fishing. A pond on the site is stocked with rainbow trout for the annual trout fishing season. Many species of migratory birds make seasonal use of the woods and marshes here.

Take the QEW to the Highway 20 exit and Highway 20 west to Fonthill. Just before you enter the Village of Fonthill, turn north on Pelham Road, which joins Hollow Road, and continue for about 2½ miles to Barron Road. Follow signs to the St. Johns parking area.

The Beamer Memorial Conservation Area encompasses 132 acres of escarpment land. It is also part of the Conservation Authority's watershed preservation plan, in this case for Forty Mile Creek, which flows just to the east of the area and drains into Lake Ontario, a mile or so to the north. A trail (another section of the Bruce) leads from the parking lot to four lookouts along the brow of the Niagara Escarpment, offering a spectacular view of Lake Ontario and the Town of Grimsby

below. From late February through May, these lookouts provide an excellent vantage point for observing the annual hawk migration.

Take the QEW west to the Christie exit in Grimsby. Head south on Christie/Mountain Road through Grimsby to the top of the escarpment. At the top, head west (right) on Ridge Road for about a mile. You will see signs to the parking area.

Long Beach Conservation Area

includes 139 acres of land on Lake Erie. The tract is bisected by Highway 3. On the lake side are 3,000 feet of sandy beach and 300 campsites, 125 of them serviced with water and electricity. North of Highway 3 is a forest with no trails, where hunting is permitted in season.

Take Highway 3 about 27 miles west from Fort Erie to the Village of Long Beach. The conservation area is about two miles west of the village.

Chippawa Creek Conservation Area

provides camping and canoe access to the Welland River. There are 60 serviced campsites. The 366-acre site includes pike spawning beds and a manmade lake where bass fishing derbies are held (an Ontario fishing license is required). It also offers swimming, hiking, picnicking, and educational demonstrations during the summer.

Take Highway 3 west from Fort Erie for about 25 miles to Regional Road 20. Turn north on 20 and continue about three miles to Regional Road 45. Turn west (left) and proceed about 1½ miles to the entrance.

HAMILTON AREA

Canada's leading producer of iron and steel, Hamilton affords an interesting visual contrast to Buffalo, her nearest blue-collar sister city on the Great Lakes. Unlike Buffalo's waterfront—which is undergoing great change with housing and marina developments rising amid the industrial ruins—Hamilton's harbor is still dedicated to hard work. Its steel industry thrives, along with manufacturing of automobiles and heavy machinery.

Western New Yorkers interested in a comparative study should approach Hamilton from the Burlington Street exit off the QEW. Burlington Street runs along the south side of Hamilton Harbor, through the industrial heart of the city.

Royal Botanical Gardens: The 2,700-acre Royal Botanical Gardens appear to be the other major land use in the Hamilton/Dundas waterfront area—another study in contrasts. Situated on the narrow plain between the Niagara Escarpment and the harbor, the RBG feature five major separate garden areas with 30 miles of trails around and through them. It is worth visiting the RBG Center first to get the visitors' guide and map so you can select what you most want to see. (Don't try to see it all in one day!) The center also features a Mediterranean garden "under glass," other inside exhibits, a library, and a gift shop.

Other gardens include the Rock Garden (considered the jewel of the five); Laking Garden, featuring perennials and an incredible iris display in early June; Rose Garden, with thousands of varieties of roses as well as a collection of scented and medicinal plants; and Arboretum, with Ontario native trees and shrubs and "the world's largest display of lilacs" (mid-May through early June). We found the

Arboretum a particularly cool and refreshing place to spend a hot July afternoon. The Arboretum climbs up the Niagara Escarpment to the Bruce Trail, (see "Niagara Peninsula Conservation Areas," p. 101) and to its association's headquarters, housed in Raspberry House.

The Royal Botanical Gardens are open daily, except Christmas Day. There are two restaurants—one at the Rock Garden and one at the Rose Garden. Guided tours of up to 90 minutes are available to groups by prearrangement (call 416–527–1158). Admission is free.

To get there from Buffalo, take the QEW to Hamilton (the distance is about 70 miles). Cross the Burlington Skyway and take the second exit, after you cross, to Fairview. Turn left on Fairview and continue approximately five miles (Fairview becomes Plains Road) to the RBG Center, where maps to the other gardens are available.

Dundurn Castle: This Italianate villa, constructed between 1832 and 1835, is a National Historic Site. It was the residence of Sir Allan Napier MacNab, Upper Canada's pre-Confederation Prime Minister.

The mansion has been restored to illustrate the castle as it was in 1855, when MacNab was at the peak of his political career. It is fronted by a gracious sweep of lawn overlooking Hamilton Harbor and surrounded by outdoor aviaries full of many kinds of parrots and parakeets. Other features include a military museum and a gift shop.

Follow directions to the Royal Botanical Gardens. Continue west on Plains Road to the first stoplight after the RBG Center. Turn left here onto York Boulevard and continue for about a mile. You will see Dundurn Castle on the left. Parking is free but there is an admission charge.

Webster's Falls/Spencer Gorge Wilderness Area: This is another cataract formed where a stream, Spencer Creek, crosses the Niagara Escarpment. In our view, however, Webster's Falls is unique among the falls we know, due to the unexpected wildness and beauty of the trail leading to it. The trail, a segment of the Bruce Trail, follows Spencer Creek Gorge upstream for about a mile, with the escarpment walls towering up on both sides. Stone giants of broken-off caprock

lie strewn about the forest floor. You turn a corner . . . and there it is! Everything you want in a waterfall. Roar, mist, rainbow—and a slippery path you can follow to get behind the falls for total ion recharge. You'll get wet, but it's worth it.

Near the falls is a stairway leading up to Webster's Falls Park and an overlook. Many folks drive to this park, take the stairs down into the gorge and back up, have a picnic, shoot a few photographs, and leave. But we recommend you take the trail. It's about a two-mile hike, round trip. The trail is part of the Spencer Gorge Wilderness Area, which is owned and maintained by the Hamilton Region Conservation Authority.

Take the QEW over the Burlington Skyway to Route 403 West. Follow 403 to Route 8 (King Street). Turn right (west) onto Route 8 and continue for about five miles through the City of Dundas. As you leave Dundas, the road begins to climb a hill (the escarpment), and you pass under a railroad bridge. Just past this bridge there is a road on the right. Look sharp! Turn here and drive in along the railroad right-of-way. You will probably see other cars and plenty of space to park. Looking down

the railroad tracks toward the high bluff of the escarpment, the trailhead to Webster's Falls is to your left, leading into the woods along the south bank of the creek.

If you want to take the fast and easy way to Webster's Falls Park, continue on Route 8 about a mile up the escarpment. You will see the Webster's Falls Park parking lot on your right. ■

With sincere thanks to Jerry Cullen for his technical expertise in the darkroom.

To my photography students who continually inspire me, and to Bob Seyfried, whose help and encouragement has been essential to this project.

BONITA A. CHIMES
photographer

APPENDIX:
Useful Addresses

Adirondack Mountain Club*
c/o Beverly Green
250 Skyview Dr.
Arcade, NY 14009

Allegany State Park*
Salamanca, NY 14779
716–354–2535

Beaver Meadow Audubon Center*
1610 Welch Rd.
North Java, NY 14113
716–457–3228

Bergen Swamp Preservation Society, Inc.*
c/o Rochester Museum of Science
657 East Ave.
Rochester, NY 14607

Bruce Trail Association
P.O. Box 857
Hamilton, Ontario
LBN 3N9
416–529–6821

Buffalo Friends of Olmsted Parks
P.O. Box 590
Buffalo, NY 14205

Buffalo Museum of Science*
Humboldt Parkway
Buffalo, NY 14211
716–896–5200

Bureau of Toxic Substance Assessment
2 University Place
Albany, NY 12203
518–458–6376
(For advice on toxins in Great Lakes fish)

Cattaraugus-Allegany Tourist Bureau
282 Central Ave.
Salamanca, NY 14779
716-945-2034

Chautauqua County Vacationlands Association
2 North Erie St.
Mayville, NY 14757
716–753–4304

Chautauqua Institution
Box 1095
Chautauqua, NY 14722
716–357–6200

Erie County Department of Parks and Recreation
95 Franklin St.
Buffalo, NY 14202
716–858–8355

Finger Lakes Trail Conference, Inc.*
P.O. Box 18048
12 Connors Branch
Rochester, NY 14618

Foothills Trail Club*
c/o Mary Dillon
60 May Rd.
Elma, NY 14059

Letchworth State Park*
Genesee State Park and
Recreation Region
1 Letchworth State Park
Castile, NY 14427
716–493–2611

Nature Conservancy, WNY Chapter
P.O. Box 5
Attica, NY 14011

*Offers a regular program of nature study, field trips, or hiking.

Niagara County Tourism
Niagara & Hawley Streets
Lockport, NY 14094
716–439–6064 or 800–338–7890

Niagara Parks Commission (Canada)
Box 150
Niagara Falls, Ontario L2E 6T2
416–356–2241

Niagara Peninsula Conservation Authority
Centre St.
Allanburg, Ontario L0S 1A0

New York State Dept. of Environmental Conservation
600 Delaware Ave.
Buffalo, NY 14202
716–847–4590
(Call or write for hunting and fishing license information.)

New York State Office of Parks and Recreation, Niagara Region
Prospect Park, Niagara Reservation
Niagara Falls, NY 14303
716–278–1701
(For campsite reservations call 800–456–CAMP.)

Sea Grant Extension Program*
Farm and Home Center
21 South Grove St.
East Aurora, NY 14052
716–652–5453
(For information on Lake Erie recreation programs)

Schoellkopf Geological Museum*
Robert Moses Parkway
Niagara Falls, NY
716–278–1780

Tifft Nature Preserve*
1200 Fuhrmann Blvd.
Buffalo, NY 14203
716–896–5200

Offers a regular program of nature study, field trips, or hiking.

BIBLIOGRAPHY

Archaeology and Geology References

Buehler, Edward J., and Irving H. Tesmer. *Geology of Erie County.* Buffalo Society of Natural Sciences Bulletin, 21, No. 3. Buffalo, 1963. This includes an indispensable geological map of Erie County.

Buehler, Edward J., ed. *Geology of Western New York: Guide Book.* New York State Geological Association, 38th Annual Meeting. Buffalo, 1966.

Calkin, Parker E., and Kathleen E. Miller. "Late Quaternary Environment and Man in Western New York." *Annals of the New York Academy of Sciences,* 288. New York: The New York Academy of Science, 1977.

Hall, James. *Natural History of New York, Part IV: Geology.* Albany: Carrol and Cook, Printers to the Assembly, 1843. This is the classic work and still well worth the reading if you can find it.

Peterson, Donald N., ed. *Guide Book: Geology of Western New York State.* New York State Geological Association, 46th Annual Meeting. Fredonia, 1974.

Ritchie, William A. *The Archaeology of New York State.* Harrison, N.Y.: Harbor Hill Books, 1980.

Russell, Eber L. *Map of Ho-do-no-sau-nee-ga or The People of the Long House.* Compiled 1851 by Lewis H. Morgan and Ely S. Parker. Redrawn 1962 by Eber L. Russell. Most explanations of Indian place names were derived from this map. Available from: Barker Historical Museum, 7 Day St., Fredonia, NY 14063.

Tesmer, Irving H., ed. *Colossal Cataract: The Geological History of Niagara Falls.* Albany: SUNY Press, 1981.

Tesmer, Irving H. *Geology of Cattaraugus County.* Buffalo Society of Natural Sciences Bulletin, 27. Buffalo, 1975. This includes an exceptionally beautiful geological map of Cattaraugus County.

White, Marian E. *Iroquois Culture History in the Niagara Frontier Area of New York State.* Anthropological Papers, Museum of Anthropology, University of Michigan, No. 16. Ann Arbor: University of Michigan, 1961.

Histories of Buffalo and Western New York

Bingham, Robert W. *The Cradle of the Queen City.* Buffalo: Buffalo Historical Society, 1931.

Brown, Richard C., and Bob Watson. *Buffalo: Lake City in Niagara Land.* Winsor Publications, 1981.

Dunn, Walter S. Jr., ed. *History of Erie County: 1870–1970.* Buffalo: Buffalo and Erie County Historical Society, 1972.

Horton, John Theodore, et al. *History of Northwestern New York: Erie, Niagara, Wyoming, Genesee and Orleans Counties,* 3 vols. New York: Lewis Historical Publishing Co., Inc., 1947.

Lankes, Frank J. *The Ebenezer Community of True Inspiration.* Gardenville: published by author, 1949.

Larned, J. N. *A History of Buffalo,* 2 vols. New York: The Progress of the Empire State Co., 1911.

Guide Books to Buffalo and the Niagara Frontier

Banham, Reyner, et. al. *Buffalo Architecture: A Guide.* Cambridge, Mass.: MIT Press, 1981.

Kershner, Bruce. *Secret Places: A Guide to 25 Little Known Scenic Treasures of the Niagara Region.* Amherst, N.Y.: Bruce Kershner, 1989.

The Nature Conservancy: *Preserving the Best: Guide to Conservancy Natural Areas in Central and Western New York.* Ithaca, 1987.

Niagara Frontier Chapter, Adirondack Mountain Club. *Wilderness Weekends in Western New York.* Kenmore, N.Y.: Partner's Press, Inc., 1978. (2nd ed.)

Schoellkopf Museum Geological Society. *A Walker's Guide to the Niagara Gorge.* Niagara Falls, 1975.

CREDITS

Photographs

By Bonita Chimes: pp. 9, 19, 20, 21, 22, 23, 24, 25, 27, 28, 29, 33, 34, 36, 41, 42, 45, 47, 48, 51, 52, 53, 54, 55, 57, 58, 59, 60, 61, 63, 64, 65, 67, 68, 70, 71, 72, 73, 75, 76, 77, 78, 79, 80, 81, 82, 83, 84, 87, 88, 90, 91, 92, 93, 95, 97, 98, 99, 101, 102, 105, 109

By Robert Husar: p. 26

By Margaret Wooster: p. 106

Courtesy Herdman's Custom Framing: p. 39

Maps

By Gary Hahn: pp. 8, 18, 38, 50, 62, 74, 86, 96

By Margaret Wooster: pp. 30, 56

Drawings

By Margaret Wooster: pp. 14, 15, 83

PLACE INDEX